Corporate Communica

A Penning Ink Publication

Penning Ink
15636 River Side Drive
Spring Lake, MI 49456
www.penningink.com

ISBN: 978-0-9890956-4-8 (print)
978-0-9890956-5-5 (e-book)

CORPORATE COMMUNICATIONS WRITING

Corporate Communications Writing can be used for college classes in public relations, writing, communications, or business. The book is also useful for those already working in public relations, or whose job requires them from time to time to write materials for a business or organization—newsletters, brochures, ads, speeches and more. Every tactic has its own conventions and must consider the intended audience and the outcome desired.

After an introduction for readers to understand corporate communications and the use of paid, owned and shared media tactics, the book provides basic instruction in three parts. Part I gives helpful insights on writing with persuasion and purpose, the ethics of writing, and how to conduct corporate communications audits and write communications plans. Part II, the bulk of the book, offers chapters on how to write specific corporate communications tactics that are paid advertisements; materials produced and owned by an organization, such as newsletters and brochures; and shared media, including websites, blogs and social media. (For help with news releases and media relations, see the companion book *Media Relations Writing*). Finally, Part III provides instruction on evaluating the success of corporate communications writing.

Dr. Timothy Penning worked as a journalist and a public relations professional before becoming a professor. He teaches public relations courses—including corporate communications writing— at Grand Valley State University in Michigan and continues to provide public relations consulting to various clients. He has a Ph.D. in media and information studies from Michigan State University and is accredited in public relations (APR) by the Public Relations Society of America (PRSA). He is a member of the PRSA College of Fellows and the Arthur W. Page Society.

TABLE OF CONTENTS

INTRODUCTION

The term "corporate communication" can be confusing. People may assume that it refers to the communication emanating from large corporations. While it includes that, "corporate" also has the meaning of a group or entity acting as one. It is in this sense that we consider corporate communications—the organized, coordinated and cohesive communications of any organization, be it a business, nonprofit organization, or unit of government.

Corporate communications is an aspect of public relations, and can also be seen as its output. Public relations is about building and maintaining relationships of mutual benefit between an organization and all of its various publics, be they customers, employees, investors, donors, voters, volunteers, suppliers and more. While much goes in to the relationship work of public relations, the communication tactics and the associated strategies that go with them are an important and most visible part of what we call corporate communications.

One way to think about the vast array of potential tactics that are part of corporate communications is to consider the PESO model. PESO is an acronym for Paid, Earned, Shared, and Owned. Paid tactics include advertisements, since we must pay for the space or time it takes to accommodate the ad. Earned media refers to media relations, since we must convince, i.e. earn, the attention of journalists to cover the story ideas we present to them in news releases, pitches and other media relations tactics. (Earned media tactics are covered in my separate book *Media Relations Writing*). Shared is all about digital media, including blogs, websites, and social media, because audiences in this digital and interactive environment may choose to share the content with their own networks. Owned media refers to those tactics that are under the complete control of an organization—we do not need to pay for placement, convince journalists to do a story, or depend on users to share the content. Owned media includes brochures, newsletters, direct mail, annual reports, speeches and other tactics fully written, produced and distributed by an organization. This book covers the paid, shared and owned tactics.

One important point about corporate communications is that it must be planned, coordinated and strategic. For that reason, Part I of this book will focus on persuasion, ethics and communication audits and plans. It is a novice and, frankly, annoying statement to say that "we just need to raise awareness" or "we need to get the word out." Both of those expressions reveal a naive belief that mere information will result in achieving something of benefit to an organization, be it sales, reputation or change in public opinion on a social issue. In reality, it is rarely enough to just provide information. People need to be persuaded to change their minds and motivated to take an action. The chapter on persuasion makes practical the most common theories of persuasion. Coupled with that, however, is a chapter on ethics, because there is a line between honest persuasion and manipulative or deceptive communication. It is important to write in the way that remains within ethical boundaries and does not descend to propaganda.

All professional public relations is done with clear objectives, and that includes writing corporate communications tactics. Good objectives are not about what we will do, but about what the public or audience will do in response to our communication—these are called "outcome" objectives. The best objectives are about positive response in terms of the overall organization and can include anything from increase in sales, donations, volunteers, brand preference, taking action on an issue, voting a specific way, and more. Part I ends with a chapter about how to apply objectives when conducting a communication audit of current communications and when doing a communication plan for the future.

Part II of the book includes individual chapters about how to write each specific paid, shared, or owned tactic of communication. Part III offers concise instructions on how to evaluate whether or not corporate communications efforts are successful.

Part I—Persuasion, Ethics and Planning

Successful corporate communications writing requires effort, strategy, thought, integrity and foresight.

CHAPTER 1: PERSUASION

People are not all the same. And each individual can vary over time. This makes persuading people a challenge. However, there are some well-founded theories of persuasion that can help when writing to a specific group of people for a specific purpose. This chapter will provide a concise explanation of some key persuasive theories and concepts, with suggested writing strategies for each.

Some may be intimidated by theory or see it as abstract and impractical. Remember, a good theory is rigorously developed and shown to be reliable in tests with large samples of people. Understanding and applying theory is therefore very practical and sound strategy, providing ideas and guidance for writing.

Theory = Strategy!

At its most fundamental, persuasive writing is dependent on the quality of the writing itself. It starts with grammar, and also includes clear structure, logical organization, and thoughtful and appropriate word choice. Those are the givens before getting into persuasive theory. If writing lacks these basic qualities of good writing, an audience is less likely to be persuaded.

Another fundamental principle of persuasive writing is to consider the basic communication model: get the right **message** through the right **medium** to the right **audience** for the intended **outcome**. It is important to always be mindful of each before and during the writing process. What exactly is it you want to say? Which communication channels or tactics are appropriate for the specific public you want to reach? And what is it you want them to do in response to what you have written?

When writing persuasively, it is also wise to consciously choose the right style, tone, and voice for each particular tactic, given the subject, audience and purpose.

• Style = the unique manner of expression. For example, formal or informal, informational or conversational.

- Tone = the attitude taken toward the audience. For example, insistent or conciliatory, an ally or an adversary, familiar or unfamiliar, internal or external audience. Is the writing oriented to the reader or from the organization?

- Voice = how you will be heard and understood. For example, institutional or personal. There is also the grammatical first (I/we), second (you), and third-person voice that should be intentional and consistent.

One final consideration before looking into specific theories is that the tactic comes last. That means before launching into writing, we must always be mindful of the larger context. This starts with organizational vision and mission, then moves to organizational objectives, which leads to the strategies to achieve those objectives, and finally to the tactic (writing). If we just start writing, we only achieve information, not persuasion or writing with a clear purpose. But, we can do that with the application of theory as strategy in our writing.

Social Judgment Theory

The essence of social judgment theory[1] is that messages produce change through judgmental processes and effects. In other words, the persuasiveness of our writing depends a lot on the way the recipient evaluates it. And what readers evaluate is not the quality, or style or creativity of our writing—they evaluate the position we take in our messages and how we take that position.

A key concept in this theory is **"latitudes."** If you think of a globe or a map, there are lines of longitude (the north-south lines) and latitude (east-west). Taken together, longitude and latitude help us determine a position on the globe. That global position makes more sense when considered relative to other positions on the globe.

In Social Judgment Theory, it is a given that there are several potential "positions" on any given topic or issue. Just as in the geographic example above, people's attitudes about a position you may be advocating is evaluated relative to other positions about which they are aware. Given this, people don't simply agree or disagree with the position you are trying to persuade them to adopt. Rather, their

---

[1] Brehmer, Berndt. (1988) Chapter1: The development of social judgment theory. In Human Judgment: The SJT View. Berndt Brehmer and C.R.B. Joyce, eds. Advances in Psychology, 54, pp. 13-40.

assessment of your position falls into a range, or latitude of either "acceptance" or "rejection."

   •*Latitude of acceptance = range of positions on an issue seen as acceptable*

   •*Latitude of rejection = range of positions on an issue seen as unacceptable*

Consider the example of an issue like immigration. People are not simply "for" or "against" immigration. Opinions are nuanced and complex. This can be seen not just in attitudes about the topic but more specific policies proposed to deal with it. See how specific policies fall within a latitude of acceptance or rejection:

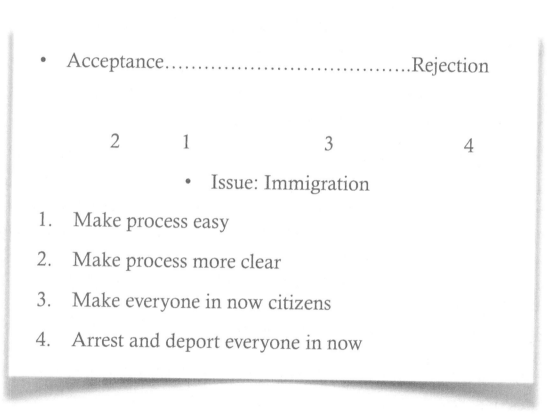

- Acceptance......................................Rejection

     2   1   3   4

            • Issue: Immigration

1. Make process easy

2. Make process more clear

3. Make everyone in now citizens

4. Arrest and deport everyone in now

Another concept in Social Judgment Theory is **ego-involvement,** which means a person's stand on an issue is central to their sense of self (i.e. ego). To take the example above, if a person is an immigrant or from a family that recently immigrated, or believes they have been strongly affected by immigration either negatively or positively, they will have more than a casual interest in the subject. They will be high in ego-involvement.

This is important because as the degree of ego-involvement increases the size of the latitude of rejection also increases. So, more positions proposed to such a person will fall into the latitude of rejection, and only proposals in their narrow latitude of acceptance will be able to persuade them. Put bluntly, it is much more difficult to change the minds or rally support for people with a high ego-involvement because they evaluate your writing not just on your arguments alone but how closely they appeal to their identity or sense of self.

Because people evaluate positions relative to others or their own, Social Judgment Theory also points out the phenomena or effects of **assimilation** and **contrast**.

- *Assimilation effect = person perceives message to be advocating a position closer to their own than it actually does*

- *Contrast effect = person perceives message to be advocating a position farther from their own than it actually does*

Note that it all depends on reader *perception*. A message perceived in the latitude of acceptance is more likely to be assimilated as the same as their own view even if there is a slight difference. A message perceived in the latitude of rejection more likely to be contrasted with their own view even more than it is.

Unfortunately, many unethical writers may use this knowledge to exploit perception to win over people to a specific position. This is why some communicators employ "purposeful ambiguity." Or, writers can unintentionally cause readers to "overreact" to a message by not writing carefully. To avoid the effect of inaccurate assimilation or contrast, clarity of writing is key to avoid chances of misperception.

Writing applications

- *Don't present your position in isolation. Consider it relative to other positions your reader may be aware of and consider.*

- *Don't try to persuade to a fixed, black and white position; present ideas within a range of acceptance.*

- *Appeal to readers' ego-involvement, sense of self, or identity.*

- *Write clearly to avoid assimilation or contrast effects.*

Cognitive Dissonance Theory[2]

Cognitive, relating to cognition, essentially means acquiring knowledge or understanding, or even more basically, thinking. Dissonance is a term from music and describes the opposite of harmony. In other words, something is "out of tune," clashing or at odds with something else.

So, cognitive dissonance is a condition when someone has two opposing or clashing ideas in mind at the same time. The writer F. Scott Fitzgerald is commonly credited with saying something to the effect that the ability to hold two ideas in mind at the same time and still function is the definition of intelligence. However, in persuasive writing, cognitive dissonance can be a barrier.

This is because, generally speaking, people seek to maximize internal psychological consistency. Put another way, people want to avoid what some psychologists cause "cognitive pain" resulting from conflicting ideas or thoughts. Because of this, people try to resolve the "problem" of two opposing ideas in their minds by rejecting one of them. Often, they reject new ideas or messages in order to maintain their current attitude or disposition.

The size of the problem, also called the "magnitude of dissonance," is affected by the complexity of the opposing ideas. The more complex or nuanced each idea is, the greater the cognitive pain. This is why some people try to simplify concepts or just avoid thinking about an issue altogether. At the same time, the dissonance is greater the more the issue has personal relevance or importance to an individual.

Cognitive Dissonance Theory points out that people will selectively pay attention to information that confirms their current mindset. They also will quickly reject or not even pay attention to new information seen as contradictory to that mindset.

---

[2] Festinger, Leon. (1957). A theory of cognitive dissonance. Evanston, IL: Row & Peterson.

Strategic writers will take into account that their intended audiences may have pre-dispositions or existing attitudes with which their message will conflict. It is important, therefore, not just to simply present a position. Rather, a writer will need to present a position in a less "painful" way in order for readers to give it some consideration. Writers should encourage people not to merely consider a different idea, but to start from square one and re-evaluate their opinion, putting two ideas on an even plane—i.e. not current vs old idea but one versus another worth equal consideration. It is also important strategically to keep communicating to audiences who already agree with a position to bolster it and avoid attitude or opinion change from contrary messages.

Another strategic consideration is the weak and temporary effect of incentives or attempts to induce compliance, such as coupons or other attractive promises to those who change their mind or behavior. A one-time behavior is not indicative of attitude change.

Yet another facet of Cognitive Dissonance Theory has to do with consistence of thought and behavior. Many people think one way and act another. This is true on everything from health behavior to purchase intention to acting on a promise to support a cause. Exposing this "hypocrisy," a form of cognitive dissonance (thought vs. action) can lead a person to seek consistency by changing either their thought or behavior. Writers need to be careful to move people in the right direction and not to offend when exposing hypocrisy—persuasion should be encountered as a helpful nudge and not an accusation.

Writing applications

- *Encourage square one evaluation of equal alternatives*

- *Reaffirm positive attitudes*

- *Expose reader inconsistency of thought and action*

- *Appeal to personal relevance and importance of issue*

Reasoned Action Theory

In the reasoned action theory[3], the *intention* of a person to behave a certain way is the key concept. And a person's intent to take an action is based on four things:

1. *A person's attitude toward the behavior.* If they consider doing something, are they thinking positively or negatively about it? Buying a car, quitting smoking, attending an event, registering for a seminar—all of these are things a person may be positively or negatively inclined towards. Obviously, a positive attitude would more likely lead to actually doing the considered behavior and may only need a nudge, while a negative attitude would require more persuasion.

2. *Injunctive norm.* This theoretical term quite simply means that a person is persuaded in part by whether they think that people important to them want them to do a certain behavior. For example, my spouse wants me to buy this car, my friends want me to quit smoking, my co-workers want me to attend this event, and so on are persuasive ingredients to someone's consideration.

3. *Descriptive norm.* Unlike considering whether other people want them to do something, the descriptive norm involves someone thinking about whether others do the behavior themselves. So for example, others have bought the same car, others have quit smoking, others have registered for an event. It is a form of "peer pressure," but it also just shows the behavior being considered is "normative", not something uniquely unusual, and therefore easier for a person to do.

4. *Perceived behavioral control.* When considering whether to do a behavior, the Reasoned Action Theory says a key factor is that. Person's own feeling of "self-efficacy," or that they are able to complete the task or successful do the behavior under consideration. If they don't feel capable or perceive the behavior as too difficult to accomplish it will be harder to persuade them to do it.

Persuasion can be a little complicated because all four of these factors may apply, but they are weighted differently (i.e. more or less important) on any given

---

[3] *Fishbein, M. & Azjen, I.(1975).Belief, attitude, intention and behavior. Reading, MA: Addison-Wesley.*

issue. The strategy then would be to appeal in writing to the factor that is likely most important on any issue, or weave several or all into a persuasive message.

Writing applications:

- *Influence the attitude toward the behavior by encouraging a reader to re-evaluate their existing beliefs about it, diminish the strength of a negative attitude and stress other beliefs about the behavior.*

- *A writer can respond to the injunctive norm by referring to it if the influential "others" are encouraging the desired behavior, or bolster an individual's independence to disregard that other if they are discouraging a behavior.*

- *With regard to the descriptive norm, a writer can make obvious the fact that others are doing the desired behavior (either with single anecdote example or a statistical number), or that others are NOT doing a behavior the writer wishes a reader to stop, such as in a cessation campaign in health care.*

- *To encourage a reader's sense of self-efficacy or potential to complete a behavior, remove actual or perceived obstacles to doing the behavior, create opportunity to successfully do behavior (physically or induce mental rehearsal, provide examples of role models or 'persons like them' doing the behavior, or offer simple encouragement.*

In essence, the keys for writers applying Reasoned Action Theory when trying to persuade an audience to take a specific action include stressing the most important influences on intentions based on the above. In addition, writers should address the most relevant beliefs affecting intentions, which may require some prior research. Different messages may be needed to those intending to do the behavior, who would need reminder and encouragement, and those not intending, who would need more strategic persuasion based on the above. Finally, persuasive writing should be done over time in a campaign, with multiple messages that encourage a planning stage and then ongoing performance of behaviors to maintain the desired action.

Trans-theoretical Models (Stages)

There are several theories or models of persuasive communication that posit that people go through a series of stages to become persuaded. In other words, not even the most brilliant writing can persuade someone instantly. Therefore, as noted at the end of the last section, it is important to consider that individuals go through a series of thought processes or stages and that good strategy would be to write persuasively for each specific stage.

The Trans-Theoretical Model (TTM)[4] combines a number of these other models and theories and proposes that people go through five stages on the way to changing their behavior. TTM is often associated with health communication but can be broadly applied. We can consider each stage and write a series of messages over time to encourage persuasion.

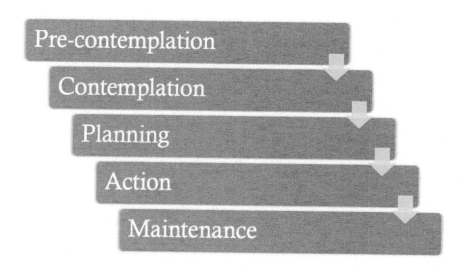

Writing application:

- *In the pre-contemplation stage, a person is not yet considering the change in behavior. To hit them at this point with heavy persuasion would be counter-productive. It is best to gently introduce them to the idea and focus on awareness about the possibility of an idea or action.*
- *In the contemplation stage, a person is thinking about the possibility of change and needs to be made to think positively about it and be encouraged in their ability to adopt the idea or behavior.*

---

[4] *Prochaska, J.O., Johnson, S. & Lee, T. (1998). The trans theoretical model of behavior change. In S.A. Shumaker, E.B. Schron, J.K. Ockene, & W.L. McBee (Eds.) The handbook ofd health behavior change (p. 59-84), Springer Publishing Co.*

- *In the planning stage, people have made a decision to change or act and need to be persuaded to actually go through with it. A message focused on encouragement and appealing to a decision already made will be most effective.*
- *The action stage is when a person actually enacts a behavior or adopts an attitude and persuasive messages should be celebratory and encouraging to reinforce the change.*
- *The maintenance stage is after an individual has made a change and must be encouraged to maintain a point of view or continue a behavior lest they be persuaded to return to prior opinion or let behavior lapse or return to contradictory behavior.*

As people go through these stages, the pros of adopting the persuasive message outweigh the cons. Also, stressing a person's self-efficacy to adopt a new attitude or behavior is more effective at later stages.

Elaboration Likelihood Model

The degree to whether or not a person is persuaded by your writing is also dependent on how hard they are thinking about the topic you write about, or how focused they are on your writing. We all think we can multi-task, or we know the difference between skimming something or really reading deeply. This is the essence of the Elaboration Likelihood Model (ELM)[5].

Elaboration in this model means issue-relevant thinking, or how hard someone processes information they receive on a given issue. This is not an either-or proposition—elaboration happens on a scale.

ELM describes two "routes" of thinking, or pathways that messages travel in someone's mind. These could also be considered strategically as two pathways to persuasion:

- *The central route*—in this route, people are focused and thinking directly about the topic at hand. In this route, elaboration is high.

---

[5] Petty, Richard and Cacioppo, John T. (1986). The elaboration likelihood model of persuasion. Advances in Experimental Social Psychology (19), pp. 124-205.

- *The peripheral route*—similar to peripheral vision, in which people see things indirectly off to the side, this is the thought pattern in ELM. In this route people are reading or hearing information you have written, but they are not giving it their full or direct attention. This often is due to the fact that the issue or topic is not perceived as important or personally relevant to them.

Again, the central and peripheral routes are not an either/or phenomenon, but they exist as extremes at ends of a scale. One is more or less one way or the other. What is helpful to writers is this: the emphasis in our writing will be more effective if we consider whether the reader will process it more centrally or peripherally.

- If a reader is using the central route and elaboration is high, then the *message content* itself is the most persuasive. This means the argument must be strong, well-reasoned and clearly and compellingly written;

- If a reader is using the peripheral route and elaboration is low, then *cognitive shortcuts and peripheral cues* are most persuasive. Research has found these cues can include credibility and likability of the message source, if the majority opinion is the same as the position advocated (ie sharing supportive statistics), a greater number of arguments or reasons to adopt an advocated view, and the length of the message itself can be persuasive. In short, people who don't want to read much will take a shortcut to make up their mind.

Central   ⟵————————⟶   **Peripheral**

Substance of message   **Cues, source, anecdote, etc.**

Writing applications:

- *If an audience is likely to be really focused on a topic because they think it is personally relevant—elaboration is high—focus on having a solid, reasoned, supported and compelling argument.*

- *If an audience may not see an issue as personally relevant or important— elaboration is low—make the issue relevant, connect emotionally, use a well-known and credible source for the message, marshal multiple arguments, and use other cues to convince people to consider and agree with a point of view.*

Some help from Aristotle

No chapter on persuasive writing would be complete without a nod to the original master of rhetorical persuasion—Aristotle.

Aristotle, and many like him in ancient Greece and beyond, have focused on three main means of persuasion: *ethos, logos, pathos*. This chapter concludes with some ancient writing applications:

- *Ethos = ethical appeal, convince audience of messenger's credibility or character;*

- *Logos = logical appeal, convince audience argument is based on reason;*

- *Pathos = emotional appeal, convince audience based on their feelings.*

Checklist for Persuasive Writing:

☐ Grammar—punctuation and sentence structure are correct;

☐ Originality—no cliche's, jargon, platitudes;

☐ Appropriate—style, tone and voice relate to the purpose and audience (see below);

☐ Targeted—writing is implicitly and explicitly tailored to a specific public(s);

☐ Objective—the writing has an apparent purpose beyond mere information;

☐ Persuasive—there is a clear strategy in the writing intending to change attitudes and motivate behaviors.

For more about persuasion, consider the book Persuasion: Theory and Research by Daniel O'Keefe, 3rd edition, 2015, published by Sage.

CHAPTER 2: ETHICS

The preceding chapter was all about persuasive writing. That means intentionally trying to change people's minds or behaviors. For some, this crosses an ethical line.

But that depends on the intent and the method of the writer.

For example, some question if persuasion is ethical. Some equate persuasion or public relations with propaganda, which certainly has a negative connotation ever since government information efforts during the two world wars.

It's an important issue to consider. But some clarity on the matter will help corporate communications professionals know if they are writing honest persuasive materials or crossing an ethical line into something that might be called propaganda.

A quick background. It may come as a surprise to many that the term "propaganda" was originally a "holy" term! In 1622, Pope Gregory XV created the "Congregation for the Propagation of the Faith." It was essentially a Roman Catholic missionary effort, and "propaganda" meant to spread the news or information about the beliefs of the church. Regardless of one's religious beliefs or affiliation, this form or "propaganda" can hardly be considered with the same disdain the term generates today.

For that, we have to go to the early 1900s when the world endured two world wars. Governments of several nations, including the United States, set up offices of propaganda to maintain public support for their war efforts. Propaganda in a negative and even evil sense is often associated with Hitler's Germany, and in particular his friend Joseph Goebbels who had the post Minister of Public Enlightenment and Propaganda. The reason propaganda is considered negatively is the means by which it was carried out with intent to deceive the public. Scholars have identified seven questionable techniques of propaganda:

Different Propaganda Techniques & Examples of Propaganda[6]

---

[6] Lee, A.M. & Lee, E.B. (Eds.)(1972) *The fine art of propaganda. Octagon Books.*

1. Bandwagon Propaganda—the appeal that everyone else is thinking a certain way or doing something;

2. Card Stacking Propaganda—only using information that supports an argument and ignoring other information;

3. Plain Folks Propaganda—appealing to people as if being just like them, even if not;

4. Testimonial Propaganda—using a popular person to carry a message because they will be more persuasive (this is common in modern advertising and influencers on social media, but must be legitimate to be ethical and effective);

5. Glittering Generalities Propaganda—overgeneralizing or oversimplifying something with positive characteristics to gain compliance as opposed to acknowledging complexity and nuance of issues;

6. Name Calling Propaganda—this is often referred to as personal attack or 'ad hominem' attack (see logical fallacies below);

7. Transfer Propaganda—transfering very positive or negative aspects of one thing to an idea, person or organization in order to 'brand' them and gain approval or rejection from an audience.

It doesn't help the public relations profession that Edward Bernays, a self-described father of public relations, wrote a book in the 1920s with the title "Propaganda." His emphasis was that communications, or public relations as it was becoming called, was more than one-way distribution of information. It was more of a social science that needed to be done strategically.

The fact that people are thoughtful and complex, as are topics and issues about we which write, is true. It is also true, then, that corporate communications must be more than basic information—it must be persuasive. However, the manner in which we persuade is vital.

People may argue that Bernays, and by implication public relations, are mere propaganda and thus unethical. However, to cast aside an entire profession with over-generalized assumption of individual intent is itself a form of propaganda, most notably name calling and transfer.

The issue can be resolved with a look at the actual distinctions between public relations and propaganda as taught and practiced by legitimate professionals today.

In a nutshell, propaganda has a connotation of "win at all costs" communication, where the intent is to control communication and persuade with any means available, whether honest and ethical or not.

Public relations, by comparison, is about mutually beneficial relationships. Persuasion of those publics with whom an organization has relationship may happen, but is is done ethically as a form of honest advocacy. It is about dialogue versus manipulation. The graphic below helps illustrate the distinction.

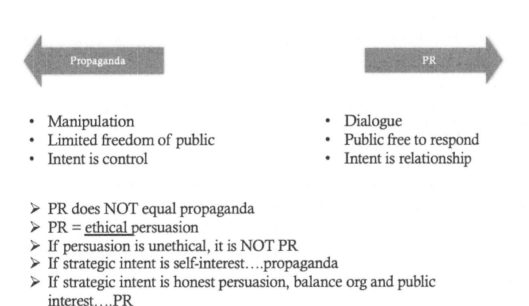

- Manipulation
- Limited freedom of public
- Intent is control

- Dialogue
- Public free to respond
- Intent is relationship

➤ PR does NOT equal propaganda
➤ PR = ethical persuasion
➤ If persuasion is unethical, it is NOT PR
➤ If strategic intent is self-interest....propaganda
➤ If strategic intent is honest persuasion, balance org and public interest....PR

Principles of Ethical Persuasion

If persuasion is to be ethical, there must be some guidelines that make it so. While entire volumes have been written on ethics, and about communication or discourse ethics in particular, we can summarize some principles of ethical persuasion to consider in corporate communications writing.

First, ethical persuasion gives an audience an **equal chance** to initiate dialogue, challenge assertions, and interpret meaning. In a corporate communications context, this has also been called the two-way symmetrical model[7] of public relations, in which publics are treated with respect and as co-equals in communication, not as targets to be won or used.

Secondly, ethical persuasion implies the public has **equal power** in interactions. Public relations scholars and professionals consider this when measuring the quality of organization-public relationships. They call this concept "control mutuality," meaning the public perceives themselves to have as much power to communicate and respond as the organization. They do not communicate "at the mercy" of the organization.

A third and vital ethical consideration for persuasive communication is that it is free of manipulation, dominance, and deception. This only further clarifies the first two concepts. But a corporate communication writer can also consider whether their work is intended for mutual benefit or organization and public, and even more broadly considers the well being of society at large in what is commonly known as CSR or Corporate Social Responsibility.

Finally, a key ingredient of persuasive writing that is ethical is that it is done with full transparency. Essentially this means that a writer acknowledges either explicitly or implicitly their intent to persuade an audience. Writers should be up front about the fact that they are advocating a point of view that is contrary to what readers may already think, or they are indifferent to it, and that an effort is being made to change their mind and behavior. This transparency, by the way, also comes off as legitimacy, or an organization's right to exist, which has proven to be more effective strategically.

Logical Fallacies

A "fallacy" is a mistaken belief, or something based on an argument that is not sound. While this is a form of bad logic or sloppy writing, this also crosses a line into unethical persuasion. If reasoning is not good or clear, it can deceive an audience. Regardless of the intent of a writer, this is a form of negligence and a lack of thinking as well as ethics. Therefore it is good to avoid these fallacies:

---

[7] Grunig, J.E. & Hunt, T. (1984) Managing public relations. New York: Holt, Rinehart and Winston.

Sweeping generalizations—An example of this would be lumping all people together with one characteristic. Eg. "people in this town are all so frugal." (Note that the use of the word "so" also implies the writer sees the characteristic negatively).

- *Hasty conclusions* with inadequate support—This is another way of saying "jumping to conclusions." In persuasion, we need a large sample, more than one example or "anecdotal" evidence to convince. Eg. "The bank teller miscounted by change, so don't trust banks."

- *Non sequitur*—This is Latin for "does not follow." To say that "Michael Jordan is so good at basketball that he'd make an outstanding baseball player" is a non sequitur. Just because one statement is true, it does not follow that the second statement would be true as well.

- *Causal fallacy*—Assuming that one event caused another. I.e. "the economy is bad because we have a new president." Those who studied statistics know that "correlation does not equal causality," or that two things being related or happening simultaneously could be by chance and not connected beyond that.

- *Ad hominem attack*—Latin for 'to the person.' This means, as mentioned above, attacking the person rather than the idea or opinion. Often this is evident in politics when people assume and discuss their opponents' intentions rather than their ideas. I.e. "He only says that because he grew up downtown."

- *Circular reasoning*—The evidence and the conclusion restate each other, proving nothing. I.e. "that rich man is smart because wealthy people are intelligent."

- *False dilemma/dichotomy*—Either/or arguments that reduce complex situations to two simplistic alternatives. I.e. "to improve education you need to either hire more teachers or build more schools." There could be other solutions, and the ones proposed may not be effective.

CHAPTER 3: AUDITS AND PLANS

Before getting into the nitty gritty of writing for corporate communications, it is important to have a big picture view. It is not wise to write a single tactic without knowing where it fits in terms of overall strategy and objectives for the organization. After all, "corporate" means a group brought together acting as one, so we should ensure all tactics we might write work together acting as one.

In order to get that big picture view, it is helpful to make sure everything an organization is currently doing in the form of communications is actually working to accomplish what is intended. This is called a "communication audit." Then, on the basis of that audit, which should identify gaps and areas for improvement and addition, a corporate communications team should put together a communication plan. In other words a communication *audit* is an assessment of past and current corporate communications, while a communications *plan* lays out all corporate communications strategically going forward.

The Communication Audit

Communication audits are also called "communication effectiveness studies" (CES). A financial audit looks to see if all the numbers add up, if the assets and liabilities balance. A communication audit looks to see if the stated goals for communication are actually being met, if the goals for what to say and who to reach are actually reflected in written materials. A communication audit is also about balance in that regard.

A communication audit specifically reviews:

- *Messages*—what the organization is saying, or isn't and should. Is it clearly articulating its mission, vision, position, what it wants publics to know, think or do?

- *Messengers*—who says what and how? Are all potential tactics used? Is the whole organization visible or just its leaders? What messages come from employees and other "unofficial" publics informally?

- *Publics*---who is being communicated to, and listened to? Who is not and should be? What is the nature of the organization's relationship with each public?

- *Outcomes*—what are the results of the current communication? What are the objectives, are they being met? What should some objectives be to be consistent with organizational vision and mission?

Sometimes it is a challenge to get supervisors, clients or colleagues to agree to do an audit. Worries about budget or fears of looking incompetent are among the reason. But a communication audit should be seen as standard as a financial audit, performance review, or any other assessment of organizational effectiveness. Sometimes this is why an outside consultant or third party is more effective at conducting a communications audit than someone from the team who writes the tactics under review.

Audits are done to ensure messages are consistent and have integrity (i.e. are honest and authentic), that all publics are being reached, that the communication goes beyond "getting the word out" and actually accomplishes organizational objectives, and to get a sense of public understanding and perception or reputation of the organization.

The methods or steps in a communication audit include:

- *Materials review*—look carefully at all current communications materials and assess messages, topics, tone, public targeted, objective evident, and the persuasive writing strategy (is it persuasive, or mere information?)

- *Depth interviews*---interviews with management and personnel in an organization to learn their objectives, with whom are they currently communicating, how they communicate (with what tactics), what messages do they want to convey, is it two-way, is it effective?

- *Perception studies*--Surveys and focus groups of key publics to get their opinion about their interest in, attitude about, recall of, usefulness of the organization and its communications. This step may take time and incur more cost so some organizations may not engage at this level.

- *Competitive analysis*—compare communication tools and messages of an organization to its key competitors. Assess publics' preference for competitors as opposed to the organization. Are tactics different and more preferred or effective? What are competitors promising, how are they positioning themselves? Does your organization need to change to be distinct and preferred?

The **materials review** is the most substantive part of a communications audit because it involves a careful assessment of the writing in all current tactics. Here are some questions to ask when conducting a communications audit of everything from brochures and newsletters to social media and blogs.

- Is it apparent that specific **publics** are appealed to?

- Are there clear **objectives** (beyond information) evident in the writing?

- What seem to be the **key messages** that come through?

- Is the writing **persuasive**, what is the writing **strategy**? Also are tone, style, voice appropriate? It is not uncommon for corporate communications writing to be bland and merely informative "getting the word out." If an audit flags a lack of strategy or persuasive writing, that is a good thing because improvement can yield many benefits currently slipping away.

- Is the tactic appropriate for its purpose and public(s); are any **tactics** missing overall? This book may introduce you to some tactics not currently considered.

A good way to organize a communication audit report is to start with an introduction that simply explains what an audit is, how it was conducted and when. The next section should be a summary of interviews. This is where whomever is doing the audit gets officials and employees of the organization "on the record" about who they want to reach and what they want to say and accomplish with corporate communications. That is one side of the "ledger." The other side—the actual tactics and how they are written—must balance the stated goals. So the next part of an audit should be the materials review, taking one tactic at a time to critique on the aspects listed above.

An audit could stop here. If there is time and budget for a perception study and competitive analysis, those could be the final sections of an audit report. Regardless, at some point the audit must go from recording observations to making *recommendations*. All recommendations (addressing additional publics, adding more specific tactics, changing the message appeals, etc) could be included at the end of an audit in one section. Alternately, specific recommendations could be noted with each tactic after it has been reviewed.

Here are some example statements from communication audits that flag writing that is "out of balance" with stated communication goals or organizational mission:

> *"You stated a desire to reach senior citizens but the writing uses conventional language more suitable to a younger population."*

> *"Your mission statement indicates that you are 'warm and inviting' yet the language in your housing brochure has an institutional tone and a rather cold third-person voice."*

> *"None of your current communications is interpersonal. A speech and/or series of events would fill this gap."*

> *"None of your current tactics seem to address young mothers, who could benefit from or be affected by your mission. Adding tactics or changing the writing to appeal to this public would be appropriate."*

> *"Most of your writing offers facts, but there is no persuasive strategy. Rewriting to address target publics' current attitudes and offer more relevant appeals would likely be more successful."*

Communication Plans

Once an audit is completed, and based upon it, a communication plan for the organization can be written. Note that a communication *plan* is much bigger than a communication "campaign." A campaign is time-limited, targeted at select publics for only a few objectives. A communication plan is for all time, all publics, and covers all organizational objectives. Again, it is large in scope because it takes the big picture view. As such, it is good to review communication plans every three to five years and update to reflect changes in the organization's plans and environment.

A communication planning process can follow these steps:

- Determine who and what you are as an organization (mission/vision);

- Determine who your publics are, should be, and consider their current knowledge, attitude, action, and needs;

- Determine key communication objectives for each public;

- Determine key messages to achieve these objectives;

- Determine the best channels, tactics, to communicate to reach those publics and achieve those objectives;

- Ensure that each public is being communicated to, consider the frequency and method strategically, and know when they are being reached (Use a matrix, of Gantt chart);

- Evaluation—indicate in the plan how you will know that each objective is met.

The key to a good communication plan is to **segment the publics**. Then for *each public*, identify specific outcome objectives (a change in awareness, attitude or action), key messages, tactics, and means of evaluating if the objectives are met. A good way to ensure that a communication plan strategically and specifically focuses on each public is to summarize the plan in a chart, with each public on a row and corresponding columns for objectives, key messages, tactics and evaluation along that row for each public.

Here is a snapshot of one row from a communication plan for a nonprofit organization segmenting "potential donors." The chart would have additional rows for each public identified in the plan.

Public	Objectives	Key Messages	Tactics	Evaluation
Potential Donors	Attract and retain new gifts	Our work stays local; Giving is your chance for input	Direct mail; Annual event; Newsletter	Request for information; Event RSVPs; New gifts

Such a chart can be placed up front in a communication plan, after an introduction. Or it can be placed at the end of the plan to summarize all that has been written in the plan.

A communication plan should provide reasons and rationale, not just lists. That's why a plan should have a written portion and not only a chart. A good way to organize or outline the writing of the plan is similar to the organization of the chart. Here is an example outline structure for writing a communication plan.

Communication Plan Outline

Intro

> *What a plan is, how it was done, how it is organized*

Public 1 (Name the specific public, eg. New donors)

> *Define public, why important*

Objectives—what public should do in response to communications

Strategy/Key Messages—how public will be persuaded by writing (apply persuasive theory!)

Tactics—which tactics are appropriate for this public and why

Evaluation—how to evaluate whether objectives for this public are met

Public 2

(Same contents as above for public 1. Repeat for all publics.)

Remember, communication audits and plans are often done together, with an audit preceding a plan. The recommendations for improvement would most often be included in the audit. A plan should reflect and incorporate those recommendations and focus on what will be done going forward in communications for an organization.

Part II—Corporate Communications Tactics

Not all corporate communications tactics are the same. Each has its own form, purpose, style and function in the communication mix. For this reason, not all writing is the same. This section will give focused instruction for writing each type of tactic.

CHAPTER 4: POSITION PAPERS

There are three types of tactics in corporate communications that are related yet distinct. Backgrounders, white papers, and position papers could all be seen as a form of report, yet they are written for different purposes and thus have different styles.

- A **backgrounder** provides historical context on an organization or issue.

- A **white paper** provides expertise or valued perspective on a topic of interest.

- A **position paper** is about taking a position or a stand on a key issue.

This chapter will offer instruction on the various types of each of these, as well as guidelines for writing them.

Backgrounders

Since backgrounders are historical facts, they are written in an objective, factual manner. Often background has historical progression, and therefore they are written in a chronological order of events.

There are different types of backgrounders. They could be a profile of a person, such as a key executive of your organization. It could be the history of the organization itself. Or a backgrounder could give the context of a public issue or an incident.

The audience for backgrounders are often journalists, so a backgrounder could be in an online newsroom or part of a media kit. But other publics may also have interest in the historical context of something—everyone from employees to customers.

The tone of a backgrounder should be factual and straightforward. The purpose is not necessarily to persuade but to educate, to bring someone "up to speed" on something before they make a decision without context. Here is a proposed outline for a backgrounder, though this may vary depending on topic and audience.

Outline of a backgrounder

1. An intro that introduces the topic and explains why it is relevant.

2. Background (chronological/historical overview. Provide perspective, foundation). Bring readers up to date.

3. Current situation. (Stick to facts. Be objective.)

4. Implications. Consequences of policy, issue, behavior. (Understand public opinion and how it changes).

5. Document sources (either within the paper or at end).

It's a good idea to make a note to update backgrounders periodically if the subject or situation is something that is continuing to change.

White Papers

One goal of a white paper could be to establish *thought leadership*. This means key publics will not only think of you with regard to your own business or organization, but they will respect you as the one to look to for perspective on an entire industry, subject, or issue.

Another purpose of white papers is to serve as a means of building a database for subsequent communications. Often, white papers offer for free information valuable enough that people will want to download it. Organizations often request an email address in order for a white paper to download.

In the same way, white papers can serve as a *loss leader* tactic. Organizations "give away" valuable information to establish their credibility and expertise on something. Those who have the white paper may then contact a business later for more information or consulting, which of course will come for a fee.

Sometimes, however, the goal of a white paper has no monetary aspect. It cold simply be to educate key publics on a technical or complex issue about which they have limited knowledge. The goal may simply be to sway public opinion on a matter of public interest.

Regardless of their specific purpose, white papers include useful information and can be presented in instructional or how-to format, or it shares research findings, or expresses an educated perspective on something related to an organization's mission or industry. In other words, the writing tone is educational.

A white paper may take various forms. It could be step-by-step process instructions for a technical exercise, it could be an informed review of various options for something such as software packages, or it could discuss the merits of pending public policy. The possibilities for subject matter are vast, so the outline approach may vary. Some white papers read like reports, others like proposals. Here, it may also be useful to include photos, tables and graphs, and as with backgrounders to include a reference list.

Position Papers

Whereas backgrounders are informational and white papers are educational, a position paper is all about opinion. The tone is persuasive, in an attempt to win others to the same opinion.

A modern public relations trend is for companies to have "purpose." This means they don't just sell products and services, but they align their very business vision and mission with their social impact.

Or, companies, nonprofit organizations, and political agencies or elected officials may write position papers to explain their specific view on an issue of public interest. It is best to note that position papers are NOT about an organization itself—a position paper should articulate the organization's opinion on an issue the public is already talking about (or should). For example, Dicks's Sporting Goods should not write a position paper about why people should shop at Dicks, but they might write one about their official position on gun control. To take a non profit example, a non profit should not write a position paper about why people should donate to them. But they may write one about why drilling for oil should not be allowed in wetlands.

Position papers have multiple uses. They can be helpful to get an organizational culture on the same page on an issue—from management to employees and external publics. Position papers also can educate the news media on an issue, and may even influence editorials or lead to an organization authoring an op-ed. Position papers can also be very useful as part of a crisis communications efforts. Having position papers on foreseeable organizational issues or crisis is a wise part of a crisis communications plan.

Ultimately, position papers go beyond merely explaining or justifying an organization's stance. They are about persuading publics to agree with that stance. Strategically, position papers can be disseminated when an issue is just starting to get public attention. This helps "get in front" of or prevent emerging crises, or it inoculates the public from opposing views (people tend to hold to the first point of view if they are initially indifferent).

It is important to remember the ethical principles shared in an earlier chapter. Persuasion should be done honestly, and never in a deceptive way or such that it disparages those with alternative points of view. An argument can be strenuous, but it should be civil and respectful.

When contemplating whether or not an organization should take a stand, or which issue to address, there are three strategic considerations:

- *Purpose*—why does your brand or nonprofit exist? Get behind issues that are relevant to that purpose, and take a stand that aligns with it.

- *Culture*—connect your stand to a relevant and current moment in society. But be sure it is an authentic reflection of your organization and not just jumping on the bandwagon of what is perceived as popular.

- *Activism*—confront a controversial issue because the organizational leaders see it as a vital aspect of organizational mission, even regardless of strong opposition.

The subjects of position papers can vary widely, but here is a potential outline for position papers with some writing strategy tips:

1. State the issue and its relevance to readers clearly.

Don't assume that everyone knows about the issue, or cares about it or sees it as personally relevant. Consider also whether the position paper is raising the issue or responding to it. This will affect the tone and approach to writing it.

This is your opportunity to "frame" the issue, to stress what part or parts of this issue are what really matters most, how people should view this. For example, are taxes about providing necessary services or an unnecessary burden on working people?

2. Give background.

This is a part that is similar to the backgrounder mentioned above. But here it is important to be brief in the context of a position paper, just to educate the reader on the issue so they are prepared to understand your arguments that follow. This is where you could mention your organization's involvement with the issue, demonstrating credibility.

3. State the position clearly.

The whole point of the position paper is to state an opinion, so do so clearly and explicitly. It could be done in a title of the position paper and again in a subhead. It is important to ensure that readers understand the rationale for the opinion. Consider if readers would expect your organization to have the opinion or not. An unexpected organizational position can be attention-getting and persuasive. If people only expect you to have the stated opinion it will be an uphill climb to convince them to think the same. It can be done, but more strategy will be required in the writing that follows.

4. Show both or all sides.

There is often a debate about whether or not a writer should share or acknowledge opposing views. It would seem that bringing up an argument that contradicts the one being advocated could backfire. What if readers accept that opposing position instead of being persuaded to the point of view of the position paper? However, acknowledging opposing views can have the benefit of demonstrating a complete knowledge of the issue and an honest approach.

But here is the key to handling the opposing view—if you are going to bring it up you have to knock it down. A nicer way of saying that is that if a position paper acknowledges an opposing view, it should also refute it. Psychological research has shown that if a position is merely mentioned without refutation, readers may adopt that view. But if it is presented and then argued against reasonably, it may be addressing an objection reader has and helping them to set it aside in favor of your view. It also may "inoculate" readers against an opposing view that comes to their attention later. In other words, if you bring it up and argue against it, then when they hear it later they will realize they have already rejected it and hang on to your position if you have persuaded them. You present all arguments and explain why yours is the most logical, convincing, or simply best.

5.   Consider the audiences.

Up til now, a position paper has been expressing an organization's point of view. At this point acknowledge who may be reading it, and why they specifically should agree with the stated point of view. This personalizes it and makes it easier for readers to see a view as their own. It becomes real and not just an abstraction, thus it is more convincing and memorable.

6.   Recommendations and call to action.

If a public has been persuaded about how to think, they may have a "so what?" feeling. Don't leave them hanging. Give them something to DO if they agree with you. Perhaps they can write or call their elected officials, or change their own behavior, or simply be conscious and caring from now on about the subject.

A good word of advice is that people would rather pay attention to someone who is PROposing something and not merely OPposing something. It is more compelling to be positively for something than angrily against it (unless they already agree).

In addition to a logical and persuasive writing outline, the format of a position paper is also important.

- Label the document "position paper."

- Include the organization's name and letterhead to demonstrate it is the official opinion of the organization.

- It should be written in third-person voice as if from the organization and not any one person.

- Write a headline that clearly states a *position*, not just a topic.

  - Eg. College students should engage in state politics

- Include sources in footnotes or a reference list.

Checklist for Position Papers *(General persuasion checklist in italics)*:

☐ *Grammar—punctuation and sentence structure are correct;*

☐ *Originality—no cliche's, jargon, platitudes;*

☐ *Appropriate—style, tone and voice relate to the purpose and audience (see below);*

☐ *Targeted—writing is implicitly and explicitly tailored to a specific public(s);*

☐ *Objective—the writing has an apparent purpose beyond mere information;*

☐ *Persuasive—there is a clear strategy in the writing intending to change attitudes and motivate behaviors.*

Plus:

☐ The position is about a public issue, not the self interest of the organization;

☐ The issue is clearly stated and made relevant;

☐ The position is clearly stated;

☐ Rationale for the position is strategically presented;

☐ Opposing views are acknowledged and refuted;

☐ The position paper ends with a clear call to action and method to respond.

Exercises:

A. Find an example of a position paper online and evaluate it based on the instruction in this chapter. Note how you would improve it.

B. Think of an issue relevant to your organization, and decide what opinion the organization should have on that issue. Remember—it should not be about the organization, but about the issue. Write a position paper that persuasively convinces a targeted audience to agree with the organization's opinion.

CHAPTER 5: ADVERTISEMENTS

Advertisements are a common tactic used in public relations and corporate communications writing. They fall into the 'paid' part of the PESO model of tactics, and they can be print, radio, television, online (and mobile) or outdoor—billboards, street benches, the sides of busses and more.

Generally speaking, there are three types of ads in terms of their *objective*:

- *Investment* ads seek to get the recipient to buy a product or service, or donate to a cause. These include typical product ads, business-to-business advertising, nonprofit fundraising,

- *Image* ads are all about building awareness, reputation, branding, and positioning. Image ads are commonly about corporate citizenship and can take the form of responding to criticism or being proactive.

- *Issue* ads are cause related or and seek to advocate a point of view on a topic of public concern. Issue ads are commonly public policy related. PSAs, or public service announcements, usually are in this category.

Ad Writing Considerations

Appeal—getting attention. An ad in whatever form it is in should be written to appeal to the audience, and make an offer of some kind that satisfies a need, a curiosity or a desire (recall the chapter on persuasion). This appeal should be direct, as in clear and explicit, although sometimes a strategy is to be more subtle and indirect. Appeals can be emotional, rational or a combination.

Positioning—where do you want to be in the audience's mind? Positioning means where you are in the minds of the audience relative to the competition. You can position a company or nonprofit, a product or service, or a certain opinion on a social issue. This requires a strategy that describes the organization or product or topic in terms that get audiences to think about it in a specific way. A position could be most affordable or best quality, or it could be most popular opinion or a well-researched perspective.

Response—objective for the audience of an ad. Any ad should be written to lead the audience to a specific response. The best ways to do this in brief ad copy is to target option leaders, anticipate the response (or resistance) to the ad, end the ad with a specific call to action, offer the means to respond such as a number to call, website link to gain more information or other appropriate method.

All of these considerations can be accomplished in ad copywriting in something called the strategic message plan, which includes 10 steps. Often these steps are included in what an advertising agency calls a 'creative brief,' which is an account executive's summary of a client's needs for the creative team. We are focusing primarily on writing and the message. Even though advertising copy can be few words, it is important to consider each of the following that apply and choose words strategically.

1. Advertising goal—what is the goal of the ad in terms of changed public awareness, attitude, or action?

2. Key organization facts—what is important for the audience to know about the organization?

3. Key features—what is unique about the product, service, cause, event, policy or whatever else is the subject of the ad?

4. Target audience—which specific public or publics do you want to see the ad?

5. Benefits—Go beyond features (#3) to describe how they will benefit, relate to, or be of interest to the target publics.

6. Direct competitors & brand image—how can your writing set you apart from any other organization that offers the same product/service or is engaged on the same issue/cause?

7. Indirect competitors & brand image—same as above, but think broadly about with whom you and your organization compete for attention, resources, recognition.

8. Product brand—not only do organizations have a brand, so do "products" or whatever it is your organization offers. How can you write about it that sets it apart from similar products or services from a company or nonprofit?

9. Strategic message promise—ultimately your message can not be about what the publics can do for you, but how you will benefit them. What implicit promise to the public is in your writing?

10. Supporting evidence—ads are said to make "claims". What is the evidence for your claim beyond merely stating it?

Ads can appear in various media—print, radio, television, outdoor (billboard, bus, park bench, etc.) and online. There are specific considerations when writing ads for each medium.

Print Ads

Print ads include a variety of ingredients to include, if they help meet your creative objective. These include:

• A visual, such as a graph or photo. Usually these are effective to get attention and draw someone into an ad to actually read the copy.

• A headline and potentially a subhead. Again, these state the purpose of the ad or creatively appeal to audience curiosity to engage the ad.

• A 'swing line' is a line of copy that connects the headline to the copy. It is a form of transition from headline to body copy. For example, a headline can make a shocking statement or ask a compelling question. A swing line can resolve that briefly, and the body copy offers explanation or elaboration.

• Body copy is the main part of the ad, which can be a sentence, paragraph or longer depending on format, medium, and creative decisions.

• A 'zinger' is a final line of copy used for creative emphasis and to add memorability to the ad. It can be a bold claim, a compelling question or some other substantive information that will strike the reader.

- Call to action. This is the explicit statement of what a reader should DO after reading the ad. It answers the "so what?" question and can be as simple as where to call or a website to see for more information, or a more directive command such as "order now" or "write your congressperson."

- Logo, slogan, tag line. This simple graphic device in image or text helps with brand recognition over time and make clear the "author" of the ad.

- Mandatories. Don't let the creative effort in all of the above cause you to leave out the mundane but mandatory information, such as a date of an event, a web address or other basic information a reader would need or wonder about.

Radio ads

Radio ads these days can be written for traditional (terrestrial) radio as well as satellite, internet or app radio outlets including Spotify and Pandora. In some cases, consumers can have a paid version of radio in order to *avoid* ads! Part of the reason for that is the general perception that radio ads are "clutter" in the listening experience. Therefore, a key strategy is to work to ensure a radio ad offers "utlility" or is useful to the listener.

Beyond making the content useful, radio ads need to consider the fact that they are heard and not seen or read. The copy needs to appeal to the ear, recognize that the ads are transient and are heard and gone in a matter of 60, 30, or even 15 seconds.

Some ads are scripts that can be read by a disc jockey or other radio announcer live on the air. Obviously, these are simpler and mere announcements. Other ads can be pre-produced with creative voiceover of more than one "actors" in roles, accompanied by side effects.

For example, instead of an announcer reading the features and price and where to order bottled water, an ad could feature two co-workers in an office discussing water, with one touting the reasons they switched to the featured brand of carbonated water. Sounds of a bottle opening and water fizzing over ice could be used.

Since radio ads are fleeting and only heard, a well-written radio ad can get attention through sound effects, a bold claim, or a a creative and interesting dialogue between two actors. Making radio ads more memorable means keeping it simple and repeating key phrases.

As for "writing for the ear", radio ads should use short, simple words and sentences. Too many multi-syllable words or compound sentences with commas setting off clauses and phrases. It is possible to use them, but it requires excellent narration to get the nuances of a pause just right. Therefore, use big words and compound sentences sparingly.

Television ads

Television ads follow the same rules of radio ads because they are transient in nature and typically are 30 or 60 seconds in length. In addition, TV ads have a visual as well as audio component. The visual could be live action with human actors, animated, or still images with text on a screen or some combination. Keep in mind that a "television" ad could also run on a website or a TV station, another site, or your own YouTube channel.

A storyboard.

Television ads can be written in two ways—a storyboard or a script. A story board is a visual summary of the ad, with a series of frames illustrating what would be seen in an ad in sequence. The voiceover or text can be below each frame.

A script that has two columns—audio on one side and a description of the visuals on the other. The visual descriptions should line up with the audio that should be heard while the visuals are seen. When

TV ad script format.

writing, it is important to consider the viewer's perspective as they engage two senses viewing and listening to the ad. Timing is important.

Outdoor ads

Outdoor advertising, be it a billboard, bus, park bench or other creative installation, must be brief. That is because in most cases, people are moving quickly past the ad. Outdoor ads usually include a large, compelling photo or image with minimal, creative copy that gets to the point quickly.

A typical billboard.

Online ads

The goal of ads on the web is to drive traffic from the site where the ad appears to an organization's own site. Therefore, the ad usually includes a graphic, minimal copy, and a link—either hypertext or hypergraphic—to your own site. Because ads online tend to annoy and interrupt an audience, there are many types of web ads that are appropriate depending on the public, the purpose, and the site where they might appear:

• Banners = horizontal, top or bottom of screen

• Skyscrapers = vertical banners

• Boxes = rectangular, not top/bottom

• Coupons = dashed border, look like paper coupons

• Pop-ups = cover part of the screen

• Pop-unders = in new tab or on desktop under browser

• Floaters = moving copy and/or graphic

- Interstitials = take up whole screen for 15 secs

- Frames = ads that take up top, left and right of page

- Curtains = roll down and then back up

- Rollovers = ads appear as mouse rolls over area

- Pre-rolls = video ads that play prior to a video

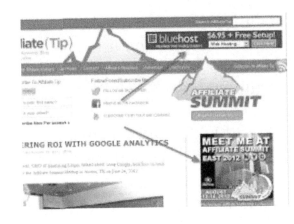

Web ads come in various forms.

When writing web ads, consider the interactive nature of the medium. It is important to be brief, and also to be interactive with content linking back to your own site. Being relevant is also key in an online environment, which is a function of placement of the ad. You can be helped by the person who sells ads on the site you've targeted to match key words in your ad to related text on your site.

Of course, this brings up *search advertising*. The ad should be written as an answer or result to a search someone has entered. It is important to write the ad using the words that someone would have entered in the search. This is known as Search Engine Optimization (SEO) and can be done using keywords. Google keyword planner is a paid service to help find the words people actually use to search. But Google Trends is free and can also help you write the relevant words in your ad copy. You can also do a search for free keyword tools.

To place your ad near relevant content, you can use Google Ads, which is a service that places your ad online near relevant content. You can do the same when buying ads on social media platforms such as Facebook, Twitter and others.

Social media ads are written to look like the posts around them. This is called "native advertising" because the ad looks like "native" content. They are also called sponsored posts and need to be labeled as such for ethical and legal reasons. Also, it is important to write these posts in a way that is more conversational than promotional. Research on the "conversational human voice" shows that this form of writing is more attractive and memorable than an institutional voice, and this is especially true of social media where people go for conversation, information and entertainment and not to be hit with a hard sell message.

Note that there are some unique forms of ads within social media platforms, especially Facebook. These include carousel ads, which are like a set of frames that a user can scroll through and experience a linear story. Or there are instant experience ads, in which a user can click within the ad and be taken to an experience still within the Facebook ad. An account with Facebook Business Manager or other social media platform business accounts is required for these features, but that opens up options for enhanced creativity in writing ads.

Checklist for Ad Writing *(General persuasion in italics):*

☐ *Grammar—punctuation and sentence structure are correct;*

☐ *Originality—no cliche's, jargon, platitudes;*

☐ *Appropriate—style, tone and voice relate to the purpose and audience (see below);*

☐ *Targeted—writing is implicitly and explicitly tailored to a specific public(s);*

☐ *Objective—the writing has an apparent purpose beyond mere information;*

☐ *Persuasive—there is a clear strategy in the writing intending to change attitudes and motivate behaviors.*

Plus:

☐ Does the writing offer the key facts about the organization?

☐ Does the writing explain both features and benefits of the product, service, cause etc?

☐ Does the writing make the brand of the organization and product etc. distinct from direct and indirect competitors?

☐ Does the writing make a promise to the audience to encourage response?

☐ Are claims made supported with evidence?

Exercises:

1. Search for ads in various formats—print, radio, TV, online—and critique them based on criteria in this chapter.

2. Think of your own organization and a message you'd like to advertise. Fill out all of the 10 items in a strategic message plan/creative brief that apply, and then write an ad for one of more medium.

CHAPTER 6: SPEECHES

Speeches are a very useful corporate communications tactic, particularly because they are most often given at face-to-face events and therefore have the potential to be very personal and persuasive.

But for the same reason, it is very important to consider some things that might not be relevant for other tactics. These include the setting for the speech. Whether it is a large auditorium with stage and podium, or a dinner event with people seated at tables, a speechwriter needs to consider this and how it affects the style, length, and tone of the speech.

The audience of the speech is another key consideration. Are they an internal audience already familiar with the organization, the speaker, or the topic, or are they an external audience who may be hearing about the organization or the subject for the first time. This will clearly affect word choice, the amount of background and education that must be addressed, and the level of detail and depth the speech can include without losing the audience.

The context for a speech determines how it is written.

This relates to the objective for the speech. All corporate communications tactics should have some underlying objective in terms of audience response. So what is it that the audience should think or do after hearing the speech? Is the objective simple to get them to be aware of an organization or the subject at hand? Or is it about developing the speaker as a thought leader on a topic? Maybe the speech is part of a broader effort to gain clients or supporters, or to recruit employees. Before writing the speech, it is best to start by laying out the objective.

Speech Objectives

There are three types of objectives for a speech, listed here with related strategic implications:

• Organizational objective—does the speech opportunity and content match the mission of the organization? Sometimes an invitation for an executive to give a speech should be turned down because it is not a good "fit" for the organization, or it's an "off-brand" context.

• Business objective—does the speech address and affect desired and expected business (or organizational) objectives? These might include increased sales, brand distinction, recruitment of volunteers or employees, attracting new donors, moving public opinion on a social issue, or more. The speech should be written with those motivational aspirations in mind, not just mere information.

• Functional objective—does the speech and its content fit the overall communications plan (from chapter 3)? The speech should be unique and original content for the audience and occasion, but key messages should be consistent with what the organization is communicating in other tactics.

Speech Opportunities

Speaking of opportunities, an organization or corporate communications executive can seek opportunities for key management of the organization to give speeches as part of an overall plan. This can be done by reaching out to local, regional, and national organizations and offering to provide a speaker, be it keynote or workshop speaker. Identify organization and industry events that provide the audience and occasion that would be a strategic fit for a speaker from your organization to be in the spotlight and deliver a speech related to your objectives. You could create your own "speakers bureau," offering bios and topics on which key executives of your organization could speak, and putting the information in a brochure and/or on your website.

But there are other organizations that help match speakers to occasions. Expertfile is one organization that brokers speakers and events. There are also a variety of speakers bureaus, both at the national and regional levels, who serve as an agency of sorts to offer speakers who are expert on specific topics. Event planners and conference organizers use them to find speakers, and if people from your organization are on their list, the better chance you'll have more opportunities to be represented as a featured speaker. National Speakers Bureau is one such organization.

Types of Speeches

There are many types of speeches, and knowing which type of speech obviously should affect how it is written. Again, with each type of speech, consider the overall goal and write accordingly.

• Informative Speech

The goal of an informative speech is education about the subject which the audience may know little or nothing about. Raising awareness about the organization if it is lesser known could also be a goal here. This type of speech approach is usually for a general audience, such as a chamber of commerce lunch, than for a specialized audience, for example a group of doctors at a medical convention.

• Technical Speech

A technical speech not only allows but demands information that is technical in nature, very specific on a topic, going in depth on a subject. This type of speech is likely for a highly educated, specific audience and the goal is to demonstrate thought leadership, gain credibility, establish a position in an industry, and inform or persuade a specialized audience.

• Persuasive Speech

A persuasive speech is specifically crafted to change the audience's mind and lead them to a specific decision, opinion, attitude, or action. (Chapter 1 on persuasion applies specifically in this type of speechwriting).

• Entertaining Speech.

An entertaining speech is one that may include more storytelling, personal and otherwise, as well as humor and other content and techniques that are closer to fun than serious in tone. The goal of this type of speech is to build relationships, establish an image and enhance a reputation. The immediate response may simply be knowledge and positive attitude about the speaker and organization, with more specific action objectives being achieved later.

- "Brief Remarks" Speech

Sometimes people receive a request to give "brief remarks" at an event. This could be an awards ceremony, an announcement, a press conference or other event where the remarks are in context of something larger. A speaker could be asked to make an introduction of the main speaker, welcome an audience, offer thanks, or accept a reward or recognition. In this case the speech will likely be very brief. However, as writers and politicians have said, a long speech requires a few minutes to prepare and a short speech could require hours to prepare. In other words, the challenge is to choose a few words carefully. The goal is to be moving and memorable, enhancing and advancing the reputation of the speaker and organization.

Two Speech Styles

A speech can be written in one of two ways. One is a fully written-out speech, in which the speaker reads on paper or a teleprompter every word. The other is an outline of bullet points, in which the speaker is guided by key words and topics in a logical fashion, but speaks extemporaneously on each point.

A fully written speech should be double spaced with text in a larger font, even as much as 16 pt, so the speaker can easily see it while at a podium. A speaking point approach can be a simple bullet list with a few words for each bullet as a prompt. See the examples of the same content from the middle of a speech using different approaches:

(Full Speech)

I can't stress enough the importance of early childhood reading. Research shows that students perform 68 percent better in high school if they read daily while a young child.

As a principle I have seen this. Take the examples of Mary and Melissa. Mary was read to by her parents, and soon was reading on her own. She was in our school library several times a week. Melissa avoided reading, never volunteered to read in class and never came to our library to pick out a book to read on her own.

Fast forward to high school.

(Speaking points)

• State purpose of speech

• Give statistical support

• Share personal anecdote.

From a writer's perspective, the speaking points version seems preferable because it is shorter and the hard work is left to the executive for whom you are writing who will give the speech. On the other hand, consider the pros and cons of each approach and choose the best one for the speaker and the situation.

A full speech has the advantage of scripting out every word and keeping a speaker on topic. If the speaker has a tendency to go on tangents apropos of nothing, or ramble on too long, this will help keep them on topic and on time. The downside, however, is that a speaker will appear too distant from the audience, too robotic, reading with a flat tone and looking more at the speech than the paper. This is why teleprompters are used for politicians and executives at large events, and coaching and practice are necessary to encourage the speaker to have conversational tone and inflection, as well as appropriate pace and non-verbal cues.

A speaking point approach, as noted above, looks easier in terms of total words that need to be written. But from the view of communications objective, the real advantage of this approach is the speaker looks more real, genuine, spontaneous and relatable. The challenge here is when the speaker may forget key content, not understand what a bullet point is referring to, or staying too long on a specific bullet and coming off as unorganized. Here again, coaching and practice are vital, as are planning meetings with the speechwriter and speaker to make sure both understand the content and objective of the speech.

So how do you know which style to choose? Generally speaking, it comes down to the speaker and the context for the speech (audience, topic, event). If the situation is a more formal occasion and/or the speaker is not well suited to free form speaking, then a scripted speech works best. If the situation is less formal and the speaker is gifted in speaking from the heart and connecting on a personal level with the audience, then speaking points might be the way to go.

Writing the Speech

The basic process for writing a speech involves four steps. The first is research. It is important for a speech content to offer something new, accurate, supported and interesting. Often a speechwriter will know the organization and the topic well, but some insights about the audience or the occasion can be helpful.

The second part is writing the speech with relevance. This means matching the organizational goal for the speech with audience interest. The speech should not be entirely about the organization, but should appeal to the audience and what they want to know or should know.

After writing the speech, the next step is revising. This may be something a speechwriter does on their own, but it is wise to have whomever will actually give the speech weigh in as well. This is not just about the content of the speech, but about word choices, lengths of sentences and other aspects of the speech that may be challenging to actually say.

That leads to the fourth step—recite. In other words, the speaker should actually say the speech out loud as if giving the speech. This dress rehearsal or practice session will make more obvious whether or not the speech is written for the ear and will be easy for an audience to follow and understand, or if there are too many large words, compound sentences or technical jargon. Also check the pacing and decide if the speech is too long or short in length in terms of actual time to recite the speech. As a rule of thumb, there are usually 135 words per minute for a speech.

Here are a series of tips for the actual writing of the speech:

- Say one main thing, a theme for the speech, and state it explicitly and more than once.

- Have 3-4 points on that main topic. It can be helpful to give the outline (see below) of the speech first, and then state each point again when coming to it.

- Repetition helps people remember. Think about Martin Luther King's "I Have a Dream" speech, in which he states that phrase repeatedly. That's what makes it memorable.

- Be mindful of smooth transitions from one point to the next. Key transition words and phrases such as "however," "on the other hand," "for example" and so forth help an audience follow the flow of a speech when they can't see paragraphs and subheadings.

- Write for the ear--use short, simple words; short simple sentences. Too many multi-syllable words, compound sentences or parenthetical statements are confusing to an audience.

- Vary the pace (pauses help the audience stick with you), volume, tone . You can direct a speaker to pause, speak slowly, whisper etc. with directives in brackets, eg. [Stop to look across audience]

- Sprinkle with anecdotes, surprising facts, drama, humor, a rhetorical question. All of these are good speech writing techniques that provide a break in a monotonous litany of basic information.

- Draw 'mental pictures' (detailed descriptions). Instead of writing "it was hot in Malaysia," evoke an image in the minds of the audience: "I had to take frequent breaks from writing to wipe sweat off my hands and arms because my fingers were slipping on the keys of my laptop."

- Visual aids help. It. Is distracting to rely too heavily on slides, powerpoint, props and so forth, but they can enhance an audience's experience if done well. Incorporate them into the speech by writing for example: "as the graph shows...." (See more on visual aids below).

As is the case with much writing, an outline can help guide the organization and logical flow of a speech. Putting down an outline first helps the writer fill in each section. Here's an example of a general speech outline:

Speech Outline

A. Intro--establish rapport, bond with audience (be unique, use humor).

B. Statement of main purpose of speech.

C. Develop theme(s), share structure (tell them what you'll talk about briefly).

D. Shift gears--body of speech with anecdotes, examples, stats.

E. Restatement of theme. Helps with emphasis and memory.

F. Brief conclusion—end with a quote, challenge to audience to act, thanks for interest, final anecdote or some other creative and unique conclusion that will stick with the audience. Avoid boring "in conclusion" or "in summary" comments that leave an audience flat.

Nonverbal and Visual Aspects of Speeches

Where the speaker looks, appropriate facial expressions, volume and pace, as well as gesture with hands are all vital to how a speech will be received. The SPEAK acronym is a good way to remember how to write speeches and coach speakers to be conscious of nonverbal cues and match them to words while speaking:

S—smile (when appropriate)

P—posture—how you stand, sit, walk

E—eye contact—don't stare, but look various audience members in the eye (pan)

A—animation—energy, enthusiasm, expression

K—kinetics (motion). Move from podium, hand gestures etc.

When it comes to visual aids, think about the context of the speech again. Also consider of the speech could subsequently be given as a web cast, turned into a video, or if a presentation could be shared on <u>SlideShare</u> for those in the audience and those who could not attend.

An example Prezi template.

If using slides, try to use more than just bullets, such as graphs and photos. Also, use minimal information on each slide. The key is to offer an enhancement or illustration, not project the speech. It is annoying and awkward for a speaker to look at a screen as opposed to their audience. For this reason, some speakers like to use <u>Prezi</u> because it has a more moving animation feel to it as opposed to simple slides.

Checklist for Speech Writing *(General persuasion in italics):*

☐ *Grammar—punctuation and sentence structure are correct;*

☐ *Originality—no cliche's, jargon, platitudes;*

☐ *Appropriate—style, tone and voice relate to the purpose and audience (see below);*

☐ *Targeted—writing is implicitly and explicitly tailored to a specific public(s);*

☐ *Objective—the writing has an apparent purpose beyond mere information;*

☐ *Persuasive—there is a clear strategy in the writing intending to change attitudes and motivate behaviors.*

Plus:

☐ Does the writing reflect the type of speech as well as the audience and venue?

☐ Does the writing reflect the objective of the speech?

☐ Is the speech written for the ear, considering word choice and simple sentences?

☐ Is the speech the appropriate length?

☐ Does the speech give direction for nonverbal aspects and visual aids?

Exercises:

1. Search for a speech online. A good source is the <u>Professional Speechwriters Association</u>, which has an archive of 'vital speeches of the day.' You can also search for speech scripts on Google or actual videos of people giving speeches on YouTube. Critique the speech based on the speechwriting aspects in this chapter.

2. Think of your own organization and a speech opportunity that may be offered to you, or one you would like to have for your organization. Consider the audience, occasion and topic for the speech, and write a speech. Have a speaker in mind. Do one as fully written speech and one as speaking points.

CHAPTER 7: NEWSLETTERS

The most important thing to know about newsletters is this: they are your organization's own newspaper. You should treat it as such, especially in the way you write it.

But just as newspapers can be in print or online, there are several options for how you distribute an organizational newsletter. There is the traditional printed newsletter, which can be mailed or made available on racks or handed out at events. It is also possible to make a PDF of a newsletter and post it to a website. There is also an HTML online version, or an emailed newsletter with summaries and links to the online article, or an email newsletter with text entirely contained in the email.

MEDIA RELATIONS

Students: The 9 things that matter more than GPA

Sure, your grades are important, but once graduate and hit the office, these skills far your grade from stats class.

An email newsletter with summary and link (above) and an HTML newsletter with content in the email message (right).

With a print newsletter, you need a designer (unless you are as good at design as you are at writing) and a printer. For email newsletters, there are a variety of services that can help you with format, list management and distribution. The top two are <u>Constant Contact</u> and <u>Mail Chimp</u>.

One question that often arises is whether an organization should have one newsletter that is intended for multiple publics or several newsletters, with each one targeting a specific public. The answer is it depends. For some organizations, one newsletter with *sections* of content for each public may be useful. A reader could go straight to their section and skip the rest, or they may enjoy being exposed to news from other parts of the organization.

On the other hand, if an organization has a lot of regular news for each public, or it is important to isolate and target publics separately, then multiple newsletters may be the way to go.

Criteria for Newsletters

Before launching a newsletter, it is wise to consider a variety of factors to know if you have the capacity to publish a newsletter on a regular basis, i.e. monthly, quarterly or some other schedule. Good newsletters meet the following criteria:

- Fill an UNMET need. How does it help the organization? What is not being accomplished by existing communication?

- Must have UNIQUE content, design, purpose, message. Why will people read it? Don't use a template, or if you do, alter it to meet your organization's brand.

- DISTRIBUTION must be effective. Do you have a good list of target publics? Is it better to print and mail, send e-newsletter blast, post to website, combination?

- Must be a JOURNALISTIC endeavor. Do things the news media can't, such as explain complex issues, cover things the broader news audience might not find interesting, but your publics will.

- Frequency should be OFTEN enough to maintain awareness, relationship, newsworthiness. Not so often it becomes annoying or is not read. E-newsletters not bound by time—send when there is news.

- FORMAT (design) and FORMULA (content categories) should be consistent and coordinated.

Another important step is deciding on what type of newsletter makes sense for your organization and the target public. Do you want to ask people to subscribe, a form of opting in? In some cases, a paid subscription communicates the value of the information. Or, a newsletter is a benefit of membership. You could also use newsletters to reach external audiences, such as customers or donors. Or a newsletter could be directly tied to an organizational objective, as in the case of special interest or advocacy newsletters.

Writing Newsletters

Once all the considerations when planning a newsletter have been decided, it is time to focus on writing the newsletter articles. Remember, an organizational newsletter should be like a newspaper; that means writing it in a professional journalistic style and is informative and a pleasure to read, not a marketing brochure in another format.

Here are some guidelines for newsletter writing:

- 'Formula' – A newsletter formula is like a recipe. That means it has general categories/topics of information that are consistent from issue to issue. Also called 'treatment.' The contents must be strategic, match organizational mission/objectives, and meet reader needs and interests. Think of a newspaper—it probably has different sections such as news, business, sports, entertainment. That is its formula, a set of information categories that are the same in each issue, even though obviously the specific articles are different each time.

- News style—use Associated Press (AP) style. That means headlines that are simplified sentences with a subject, verb, object, not titles or exclamations. Another journalistic criteria is an objective, third-person voice. That means no personal pronouns and no opinion. As tempting as it may be in a newsletter to boast, celebrate or persuade, remember that objective, journalistic writing is more credible and often easier to read. Using quotes of key officials or representatives of various publics allows the organization and its publics to 'speak', and in quotes opinions may emerge.

- Tell stories. Feature employee accomplishments, donor contributions, customer response etc. Stories communicate what an organization values. Narratives are fun and easier to read than declarative, promotional jargon. Stories don't just tell, they show. Also, in a subtle way, they are more persuasive because of their authenticity.

- Avoid fluff. Don't be cutesy in your tone and don't include items just to fill space. Make sure every article has a use for the reader. This takes you back to the formula—if you stay with it when planning each issue, you'll always have content that is useful and interesting to readers.

- Gathering info is vital. Be like a reporter, "work the beat." Know your organization and its news sources. Solicit info and ideas. Walk around, attend meetings, pay attention and share the news in the newsletter.

- Be accurate. Verify data, double check quotes. Run stories past sources (news reporters don't do this, but PR writers have that luxury since you work for the organization). Remember that reputation depends on being professional, truthful and not misleading in newsletters.

Consider the appeal of the newsletter article examples below. One is 'boring' and merely informative. The other is 'brilliant' because it tells a story. Also notice the complete headline as opposed to a mere title::

- (Boring):

Scholarships Awarded

Grand Valley State University gave 72 scholarships this past year. The scholarships totaled more than $20,000 and assisted students from various majors.

Every year, the university receives contributions to its various funds. Donors have the option of giving to scholarships, capital campaigns, or other specific projects.

Give to GVSU! You can make your donation online at www.gvsu.edu/giving.

- (Brilliant):

New Scholarship Helps PR Student Finish Degree

Kara VerPlank was desperate. She was considering just dropping out of college. Her father had passed away two months before. She had taken a second part-time job because her mother could no longer afford tuition, housing and other costs of her being in college. She was on her own financially.

Until a professor mentioned a new scholarship available for students in her major. She applied for the Frederick Chapman Scholarship, designated for public relations students. When she learned she was the winner, she was overjoyed.

"I cried when I read the email," VerPlank said. "This $1000 scholarship is the difference between me getting a degree or going home and working at the grocery store full time."

Newsletter Design

If the formula is the regular categories of content of a newsletter, the format is its design. The formula and format should work together. For example, if your formula calls for specific sections, the format can set those apart graphically with a section header at the top of the page where the section begins. This could be larger, colorful text, reverse text in a colored bar or some other graphic device. The formula can also be illustrated graphically in the table of contents to show readers up front what the sections are and on what pages inside they each begin.

A table of contents. Notice the black text identifies the sections that appear in each issue (formula), and the red ink identifies the specific articles in this particular issue. This design (format) is a way for the formula and format to work together.

This academic program newsletter includes four sections in its formula— program, students, faculty alumni. The header atop this page —"Program"—shows how the format (design) and formula (contents categories) work together.

Other aspects of the design of a newsletter include the banner or flag, which is the title of the newsletter. Again, make it look like a bonafide, professional periodical. The name of the newsletter can be fun and creative or straightforward, but either way it should communicate something about the organization.

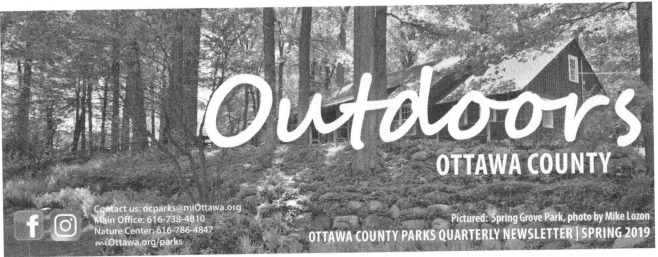

The quarterly newsletter of a county parks department is called "Outdoors." Notice the issue date and full name of the organization appear on this 'flag.' It is also possible to change the photo image each issue or keep it the same.

Another design aspect of a newsletter, particularly if it is more than a few pages, is what's called a "masthead." This is usually a box or sidebar on the first inside page that includes information about the organization, how often the newsletter is published, the names and titles of the editor and other key organization officials, and contact information. Social media addresses can go here as well.

Example newsletter masthead.

A typical plan for each newsletter issue is as follows:

- A cover that includes the most compelling article/story for that issue. You can also place the table of contents or "inside this issue" on the cover. Don't refer to page 1, obviously, because that will be immediately visible. But for everything on page 2 or following list the section with abbreviated headlines for each and the page number on which they appear. A table of contents is not required but is useful for newsletters of four or more pages.

- On page 2, include the masthead and a letter from the editor, president, executive director or some other key official from the organization. This can be first-person and more personal in tone, giving an overview of the issue and highlighting key items from the issue.

- The rest of the newsletter should have clearly identifiable sections that follow the formula, with associated articles in each section.

- Depending on design, a newsletter's back page can be blank and used for mailing information, a large photo, social media and other contact information, or additional articles.

Checklist for Newsletter Writing *(General persuasion in italics):*

☐ *Grammar—punctuation and sentence structure are correct;*

☐ *Originality—no cliche's, jargon, platitudes;*

☐ *Appropriate—style, tone and voice relate to the purpose and audience (see below);*

☐ *Targeted—writing is implicitly and explicitly tailored to a specific public(s);*

☐ *Objective—the writing has an apparent purpose beyond mere information;*

☐ *Persuasive—there is a clear strategy in the writing intending to change attitudes and motivate behaviors.*

Plus:

☐ Are the articles in AP style, objective voice, third-person?

☐ Are headlines subject-verb-info style like a newspaper, and not mere labels?

☐ Are the articles written as stories, with quotes and descriptive detail, and not just marketing copy?

☐ Is there a clear formula, shown in both the content and format/design?

Exercises:

1. Search for a newsletter online or one you have received in the mail. Critique the newsletter based on the criteria for good newsletters described in this chapter.

2. Think of your own organization and come up with a formula for a newsletter (or revise an existing one). Then write an article for a future issue that follows the writing guidelines in this chapter.

CHAPTER 8:BROCHURES

Brochures are a very common communication tactic for any type of organization. They have the characteristic of being for one specific purpose, for one or a select few specific publics, and for one-time use, as in not a periodical.

Brochures are actually a broad term for a variety of specific types of communication tactics. A brochure could also be called a:

• Flyer = single, flat sheet, often placed on cars or pinned to bulletin boards;

• Leaflet/pamphlet = old fashioned term, could be flat or folded;

• Tract = has connotations regarding content, either religious or political.

Brochures can come in many shapes, sizes and lengths. A brochure could be 8 ½ x 11, 5 x 9 or a range of other dimensions. It could be just a few pages or it could be long enough to constitute a booklet. There are many choices when it comes to size of a brochure, but it should as always depend on purpose and audience and the best way to communicate to that audience to achieve the intended purpose. Generally speaking, the more familiar or interested a public is in certain content, the more length and depth the writing can have.

However, the most common form of brochure is the 8 ½ x 11 sheet of paper folded twice so that it has three panels of content on each side. This is often called a 'tri-fold' even though technically there are only two folds. There are two ways to fold such a brochure, a letter fold or a z-fold.

A letter fold brochure.

The letter-fold brochure has one panel folded inward and then the other over top of it, the way most people fold a letter. This is best for brochures that will be mailed in an envelope because it protects the edges from catching on the envelope.

A z-fold brochure by comparison has one panel fold over the middle and the other folds not over it but in the opposite direction. The resulting brochure has the shape of a "z". The advantage of a z-fold brochure is design versatility because when unfolded the design can cover the entire page.

A z-fold brochure.

The main reason for choosing a specific design style or way of folding a brochure has to do with the flow of the content. The writing (discussed in more detail below) must work strategically with the design. Copy should be arranged in blocks, on the brochure cover, the flap and each panel either separately or together, and finally the back panel. The flow and the order a reader engages content is different in a letter-fold and z-fold brochure.

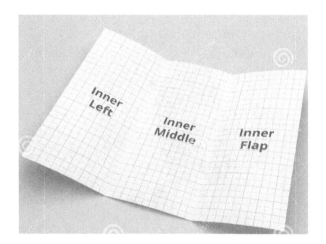
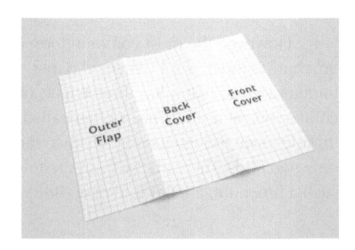

The above images show how to layout copy for an 8 ½ x 11 letter-fold brochure. The reader will engage material in this order: front cover, outer flap, inner left/middle/flap (either as separate panels or a combination) and finally the back cover. This is why both design and writing need to be considered together.

The brochure cover requires special consideration, because its design and copy will determine if a reader chooses to go inside the brochure or not. Different decisions may be made if the brochure is to be mailed, on a table or handed out, or in a brochure rack where only the top of the cover is visible. The cover should make clear to the reader what the brochure is about and appeal to reader interest. This can be done with a compelling image, but writing is also important. Brochure cover writing techniques include: a question, a compelling claim, an opportunity, a teaser, or start a story. All of the above can lure the reader to resolve a question or find out more by reading inside.

For the remaining panels, it is best to NOT let the copy flow from one panel to another. Write succinctly and keep copy in blocks that stay on separate panels, or adjacent panels on the inside. For example, the outer flap and back cover can work as one unit, and on the inner panels there are several options for arranging the copy:

• each panel separate;

• Inner left and inner middle together, and inner flap separate;

• Inner left separate, with inner middle and inner flap together;

• All three inner panels integrated as one copy and design unit.

Panels as separate units

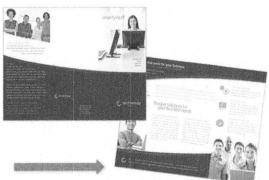

Integrated panel design

The next copy the reader encounters after the cover should answer the question, resolve the teaser, or in some way follow logically from the cover. The remaining panels could be whatever content is appropriate next, packaged in a way that makes strategic sense, and follows a logical sequence.

The back cover could be designed as a unit with the outer flap, or could stand alone since it would be seen by itself when the brochure is folded. The back cover is the best place for a call to action with contact information, of if a self-mailer (i.e. without an envelope) this is where the postal indicia, bar code, addressee and stamp would go. See a local post office or mailing service for specifications.

Brochure Writing Tips

Once a design and layout has been determined that works well with the arrangement of content, it is time to actually write the brochure. Here are some writing tips for brochures.

- Make the cover interesting with an informative headline and other copy that clearly indicates, from a reader-interest perspective, what the brochure is about and gives a reason to go beyond the cover to read more.

- Highlight the benefit to readers throughout the brochure. Don't write from the perspective of what the organization wants, but what the specially targeted public needs, wants, or is interested in.

- Be sure the writing is clearly directed toward a specific audience in the word choices, examples and information that is relevant to that audience.

- Make the copy easy to read. Use short sentences, graphically highlight important facts, demonstrate a clear organization with subheads to help readers move through and locate specific information easily.

- Write in personal terms—use the second-person 'you' language, as if the reader is the only one in the audience.

- Write on a friendly level—be lighthearted if appropriate, or if the topic is serious, use an empathetic and personal as opposed to institutional voice.

- Write in positive terms—resist resorting to scare tactics, show optimism.

- Don't be too specific with time—you could give the piece a short shelf-life if your writing mentions a specific year or says "this year."

- Make sure the writing is direct—Don't make readers guess, lead them to desired attitude or behavior. Often this involves expressions like "you should…." or "you can…."

- Increase reader interest—provide tips, concrete advice, how-to ideas.

- Highlight headlines and subheads—be more than labels, be descriptive/intriguing/informative. For example, a non-profit cause-related brochure might have subheadings: "why you should care," "what we're doing about it," and "how you can help."

Checklist for Brochure Writing *(General persuasion in italics)*:

☐ *Grammar—punctuation and sentence structure are correct;*

☐ *Originality—no cliche's, jargon, platitudes;*

☐ *Appropriate—style, tone and voice relate to the purpose and audience (see below);*

☐ *Targeted—writing is implicitly and explicitly tailored to a specific public(s);*

☐ *Objective—the writing has an apparent purpose beyond mere information;*

☐ *Persuasive—there is a clear strategy in the writing intending to change attitudes and motivate behaviors.*

Plus:

☐ The cover is appropriate for distribution method, clearly indicates content of brochure and creatively draws reader inside.

☐ The brochure is written in a way that is relevant to specifically targeted publics.

☐ The brochure is not dated or written in a way that limits its shelf life.

☐ The brochure has a call to action and way to respond.

Exercises:

1. Search for a brochure online or one you have received in the mail. Critique the brochure based on the criteria for good newsletters described in this chapter.

2. Think of your own organization and come up with an idea for a brochure that would help accomplish one of its communication objectives. Consider the target public and purpose of the brochure. Plan the size and design and how to block the copy strategically for reader flow. Then write the brochure.

CHAPTER 9: DIRECT MAIL

Direct mail can be a bit of a confusing term. It does include actual mail, as in from the post office. But today direct mail can also include digital versions. The "direct" means the purpose is more sales or appeal oriented.

There is SMS, or short message service, also known as text. Companies and other organizations are increasingly using text message to communicate with their key publics. Since cell phone numbers are not published in directories and are considered private, it is good practice to make sure recipients opt in to the option of receiving text messages. However, recent research shows that most 18-49-year-olds see texting as a preferred way to communicate with businesses.

The advantage of reaching people via text is that it finds them where they are. They could be at home or work, but they could also be in a store. With GPS and other technology, it is possible to send a message precisely when someone is near a store or other designated location.

Text messages obviously need to be brief given the small screen space and time people would want to spend reading a message on such a device. Therefore, when writing direct mail messages for text, it is best to follow the pattern of *offering some benefit and prompting a response with a link to a website* for a coupon or more information. Texts can also be to make reservations, send appointment reminders, solicit donations, and more.

Several services provide help with the technical aspects of mass text:

• The Mobile Marketing Association

• EZ Texting (the top rated overall)

• Slick Text (considered the best for small business and organizations)

• Simple Texting (offers the most flexible plans)

In addition to SMS direct mail, there is the email option. The chapter on newsletters mentioned Constant Contact and Mail Chimp as potential services to help with email newsletters. The same can be used for email marketing and more specific messaging that is not the style or length of a newsletter.

One additional service to consider for direct email is agileEMAIL by Movable Ink. This company can help create and distribute dynamic emails, or emails that change the content each time a recipient opens them. This could be useful for sports teams in which the score will be updated, or a fundraising campaign email that can show the latest amount raised.

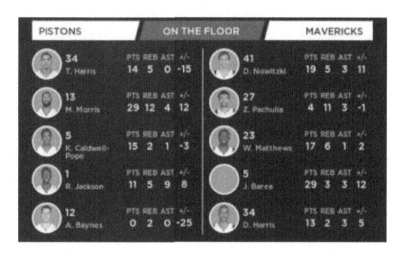

Example of a dynamic email with sports scores.

Why Direct Mail in Print

While the electronic versions of direct mail are contemporary and offer many useful digital features, direct mail on paper via the post office is still very popular. The US Post Office sent more than 77 billion pieces of direct mail in 2018, and direct mail is a $44 billion industry.

The reason direct mail is popular is because it still works. The reason it works is that people find it less annoying than marketing messages in email or text, they sort physical mail quickly, and it can seem more personal. Also, it is possible to include physical items such as examples, bookmarks or small incentive gifts.

Of course, whether or not a direct mail piece is considered "junk mail" depends a lot on the writing and whether or not the recipient sees it as relevant. You also need to pay attention to the "do not mail" list or requests to be taken off a mailing list.

There are a variety of types of direct mail letters. There are traditional sales letters, non-profit fundraising appeals, letters that advocate for a cause or inform about an issue, or those that come from a political candidate or a group trying to gain votes for a specific ballot proposal.

Regardless of the purpose of the direct mail, there are usually three components to a direct mail package—the *list, the look and the lure*.

The *list* is important and related to writing. The more specific your list of recipients, the more specific and relevant the writing can be. "General" lists are hard to write to because there can be so much variance among the recipients that you can only use broad, vague and often ineffective references and appeals.

You can buy lists from list brokers, such as <u>List Giant</u>, or maintain your own database internally. Either way, it's important to be strategic in how you sort the list for each direct mail campaign. Think of the different ways you can break down a list or sort the database:

- Sorts—age, demographics, geography;

- Donors--Recency, frequency, quantity of gifts;

- Political—Ideology, voting patterns, issue relevance;

- Sales--Repeat or prospective customer.

You can see in each of the above examples for breaking down a list how the writing would change. For example, you don't ask for contributions the same way to someone who gives a small amount compared to a large amount, or one who gives annually compared to someone who donates on a regular basis.

The *look* of the direct mail package of course relates to the design. The outer envelope is more likely to be opened if it has appealing graphics and copy in addition to the usual address information. As a rule of thumb, when the subject matter inside is more serious or complicated, a standard design approach may be the best, but there can still be some copy explaining what's inside and enticing the recipient to open it. Meanwhile, if the topic of the letter is easy to understand and/ or lighthearted, a more flamboyant design approach could work well.

A standard, business design for direct mail on the left. A more creative approach on the right.

The *lure* of a direct mail is all about an incentive or making an offer of some kind. This is done in the writing itself, which we will discuss next, but it also means taking advantage of the physical nature of a direct mail by postal mail and the ability to include items in the envelope. These can include: address labels, stickers, magnets, bookmarks, coupons, even a dollar bill. This gives the recipient something to keep in their home or office and remember the organization who sent it.

A direct mail package that included gloves as a lure.

So, the elements of a direct mail package include:

• The outer envelope, which should have an appeal in writing and graphics;

• A letter, which is the foundation and most important piece;

• An incentive or enclosed material, gift, etc.;

• A response card that provides checkboxes or an easy way for a recipient to request information, order a product, donate money or whatever action is desired for the campaign.

• A reply envelope, usually postage paid, for the response card to be mailed in.

A mailing house or the post office can help with regulations for design of a reply envelope, assembling and inserting and addressing all the pieces, and mailing it. Consider using first class stamps to look more personal, as opposed to a machine printed postage paid stamp.

A response card with a business reply envelope.

Writing Direct Mail Letters

As noted above, a teaser on an outer envelope gets attention. It can also serve as a creative theme that can be continued in the letter writing, such as repeating it in a headline of the letter and addressing the theme throughout the letter.

The format of the letter is important too. The letter should be on letterhead, have a date, include the name and address of the recipient (either individual or as married couple—however the recipient stated they prefer to be addressed), and the salutation (Dear….).

The letter should be written in a *reader-centric* fashion. In other words, don't address what you or your organization want. Write from the perspective of what the reader needs or wants, a solution you can provide them, an opportunity for them.

At the same time, a good letter needs to have an explicit call to action. At the end of the letter ask the reader to request more information, make a reservation, order a product, vote, donate, or any other objective. This can be done by referring to the response card that enables the response or direct them to a website for an online action.

The letter should end with a closing sign off, such as Sincerely, Gratefully, or some other appropriate sign off. This should be followed by the author's name, title, name of organization, address, phone and email. Consider a P.S. at the end of the letter as well. Technically this is not needed (P.S. stands for 'post script' and before computers someone would have written that because they had forgotten to write something before they signed the letter). These days, a PS is good to use as a reminder, an emphasis of the call to action, an offer to provide more information, or some other key information for the reader.

Letters can also use creative devices. One is to personalize the letter with the recipient's name in more than just the address and salutation. For example, in the middle of a letter, a reference to the individual or something about them can be compelling to a reader who now knows the letter is not 'generic.' This is done by merging the letter with the database and inserting field codes as text into the letter. For example:

"[first name], we know you have ordered [product] before, and may be interested in our new line of accessories."

Or,

"We want to thank you, [first name], for your generous gift of [amount]."

There are actually debates about how long a direct mail letter should be. Some are four pages and have many highlighted, bold or underlined sections within it, as well as graphics and photos and pull-quotes. This may look impressive, and in some cases the content or situation may merit a longer letter. However, keeping it to one page can be a good strategy as well given that readers are overwhelmed with messages.

So, a good direct mail letter could follow this general outline:

• Headline

• Address and salutation

• Introduction that appeals to the reader's need, interest, desire

• Explanation of the opportunity

- Personalized paragraph with name and other specific detail as example

- Appeal and call to action with reference to response card

- Conclusion, thanking for attention and/or offer of more information

- Sign-off and signature

- A PS with a reminder or additional incentive or call to action

Checklist for Direct Mail Writing (*General persuasion in italics*):

☐ *Grammar—punctuation and sentence structure are correct;*

☐ *Originality—no cliche's, jargon, platitudes;*

☐ *Appropriate—style, tone and voice relate to the purpose and audience (see below);*

☐ *Targeted—writing is implicitly and explicitly tailored to a specific public(s);*

☐ *Objective—the writing has an apparent purpose beyond mere information;*

☐ *Persuasive—there is a clear strategy in the writing intending to change attitudes and motivate behaviors.*

Plus:

☐ Does the outer envelope entice the reader to open it?

☐ Does the letter have a headline and all other aspects of a good letter (salutation, sign off, letterhead etc)

☐ Is the letter reader-centric?

☐ Is the letter personalized?

☐ Does the response card enable the recipient to respond appropriately?

Exercises:

1. Search for a direct mail letter online or one you have received in the mail. Critique the direct mail package—mailing envelope, letter, and response card—based on the criteria for good direct mail described in this chapter.

2. Think of your own organization and come up with an idea for a direct mail appeal. To what specific publics would you send it? How would you appeal to them? What response would you want? Write a letter, response card, and design an outer envelope to fulfill that plan.

CHAPTER 10: WEBSITES AND BLOGS

It is hard to believe but websites were a new thing back in the 1990s, and blogs emerged not long after that. There was a time when organizations thought that having a website or blog was trendy. Today they are an expectation in the minds of many key publics.

This chapter will address writing websites and blogs together because there are many similarities in the sense that they are online. However, website writing and blog writing are very distinct in tone and purpose. So we will address them one at a time.

Websites

The biggest mistake a writer of a website can make is to copy and paste content from another tactic directly into a web page and consider it done. Web writing is different than print in ways that should be obvious by now to anyone who used a website. Yet there are still many websites that don't take advantage of the medium.

Even though websites have "pages," they are different than print material for readers in significant ways:

• They are not three-dimensional. A reader can not pick it up and flip through it.

• They are not linear. There are many paths through a website. They are—and should be—interactive. It is easy to click on a word or image and be taken instantly to additional information.

• Website content can be engaged by clicking or scrolling, not a simple page turn.

• Websites need to be navigated with more than a table of contents.

Given these characteristics of websites, there are some advantages and challenges to writers when considering online content. The advantage of the interactive nature of websites is the ability to give each reader a unique "experience" with the content. They can take their own path though a website, divert from one piece of writing to another to explore related content through a link, or chose different categories of content from the navigation bar in the order they choose. The reader is in control of the flow of content, but the writer can plan and enable that purposefully.

Writing for the web also allows a writer to reach both "divers" and "surfers" online. A diver is one who will go deep into a particular page on a website, scrolling to the last bit of content on the topic they are interested in. Surfers are those who land on a home page, then maybe jump from each page of the site from the navigation bar and reading only what first comes up. It's the difference between someone who's really shopping and someone who is "just browsing" (literally, we call the software for engaging the web a "browser").

Good web writing reaches both surfers and divers.

Another key benefit of writing for the web is that it is timeless, in two ways. One, it is available 24/7 to readers, and there is no worry about "distribution" since it is online. A second reason web copy is timeless is that it is simple to edit any information that has become out of date—price, personnel, etc. This of course means it is crucial to keep monitoring a site once published for continual refreshing.

That leads to the challenges of web writing. It's never really done. Once you click "publish" you need to set times to review and update content. This includes links to any external information if the writer of that website has changed anything.

Another challenge is the fact that the very nature of the web can be distracting to readers. The fact that they can click and go elsewhere—on your site or to another one—is tempting to them and a reality that makes it hard to retain readers (unless the writing is really compelling). Readers also may receive text messages, emails and other notifications on their laptop or phone or whatever they are using to read your web copy. When you write for the web, you have more competition.

An internal challenge is that a web writer does not control all of the content. Maybe you are only allowed to write for a few pages, or even if you write the whole site you may have arguments from others about what goes on the home page, what is more prominently featured in the navigation bar, and other content struggles.

Finally, as easy as we think it is for someone to search for and read content on your website, there are challenges to readers when online that translate into writing challenges as well. Consider what research says about how people read differently on a computer:

• They read 25% slower on the web than on paper;

• They experience eye fatigue;

• They move around quickly and have little attention span;

• They hate overly hyped language;

• They have easy alternatives for content.

The way web writers can respond to these realities readers face online is to cater to what readers want, in terms of content and the overall online experience. Research from search engine data and user surveys has also shown that readers want the following from websites:

• Help with a specific tasks. ("how to…" is good web copy);

• Information that fits their perception;

• The ability to search a website (so have a search field on your site);

• Ease of navigation (so have an intuitive navigation bar);

- No waiting (graphics and videos and other fun features may look good to you but slow down load time, which annoys readers or sends them away);

- Choices and control. (Have a robust navigation bar, with submenus under each item on the navigation bar so readers have quick options);

- Little or no scrolling. (Readers will scroll when they have found content they are interested in. But early on content should be contained in one screen so writing must be concise and clear);

- A mobile version. (Many, even a majority, of people engage websites on mobile phones. It is vital to ensure that your website has a mobile version (often the software used to build a website can detect whether a user's IP (internet protocol) number if they are on a phone or computer and will convert the view of the site accordingly).

User-Oriented Sites

The key to good web writing, like a lot of other writing, is to know the audience and their characteristics and interests. Since websites can be for all publics of an organization, this means deciding first who all your publics are, then designing a site that meets all their needs such that each public finds the content for themselves quickly.

What this means is using an *outside-in* approach. In other words, many organizations construct their websites from the inside out. They have meetings with key department leaders, who all offer suggestions for what should be on the website based on what *they* want to *say*, as opposed what *readers* want to *read*. A good reader-oriented site is first noticed by a navigation bar that uses terms and labels content categories according to what publics search for and not the names of departments or other organizational terminology.

 Vehicles   Shop   Finance   Owner

A reader-oriented website navigation bar on Ford's website.

Good practice with website navigation bars is to include them on every page, and also have submenus that open when a mouse cursor scrolls over. This way a reader is never more than two "clicks" from content anywhere on the site.

Another aspect of reader-oriented websites is where the copy is in "chunks" and where readers must "scroll." A chunk of copy is text that can be seen on one screen. Scrolling copy requires the reader to scroll down. As noted earlier, readers are willing to scroll when the subject is interesting and relevant to them. So, as a rule of thumb, copy on the home page or the first page of a section of a web site should be written concisely in a viewable "chunk." Copy deeper in a site that is more specific can be longer and require scrolling because the reader by then is engaged. Another way of saying that to use terms from before is that readers often "surf" before they "dive."

To take the Ford example, copy should be brief initially under vehicles, where it may mention the variety of vehicles Ford offers and some other general brand information. But once you go deeper into one specific vehicle, say the Ford Escape, a reader can scroll down to get the aspects on the particulars of that model's performance and specifications.

Once a reader is on a page with more depth of copy, it is important to write it in an interactive way. This means making key words hypertext links to other related content on the site, or even external sites (you can program it to open a new tab and keep the reader on your site or allow them to leave for an entirely different site). You can also make other aspects interactive, such as photos and graphics that link to other pages or videos that play on the page or link the reader to a video page.

Home Buying Loan Process

Whether you are looking to get pre-approved or have found your home, we can help you each step of the way. Our seasoned loan officers will assist you to determine which of the many loan options may fit your needs.

At Huntington, we are committed to giving you the individual attention you deserve. We offer you smooth, dependable service with a personal approach. This means involvement from the first step to the last, with the Huntington origination staff working according to your schedule. Below is a brief listing of what you can expect during the Huntington mortgage process.

Based on your individual circumstances, your path may vary. We invite you to stop by or call The Huntington Mortgage Office nearest you and let us show you how we take your mortgage needs personally. Generally, here's what you can expect once you apply for your Huntington mortgage loan:

Step One:

Complete your application Complete your application in its entirety. If you apply online, your application will be received instantly by a qualified Mortgage Loan Representative and they will contact you regarding any additional information that is needed and walk you through the rest of the mortgage

Which website has interactive copy?

Plan a Visit to Meijer Gardens

Explore the sights, both indoor and out.

A destination marrying world-renowned sculpture and horticultural landscapes, Frederik Meijer Gardens & Sculpture Park's indoor and outdoor gardens and sculpture galleries hold something for the whole family to enjoy.

Tours, programs and interactive activities are available for visitors throughout the year. Check the Events Calendar or the digital display sign at the admissions desk upon arrival for the day's activities.

WHAT TO SEE   SHOP & EAT   GROUPS & TOURS   HOURS & RATES   DIRECTIONS & TRAVEL   POLICIES   TOP ▲

What to See

The 158-acre main campus may take up to two, four, or eight hours to walk through depending on what you choose to explore. With a large variety of art and plants, Meijer Gardens has something to pique any interest. Explore some of the many great highlights we have to offer.

Another vital part of good writing for websites is search engine optimization (SEO). Essentially, this means writing using words that readers would actually search on, and not the jargon of your company or industry. People start their web experiences by searching, using Google, Bing or some other search engine. Your web site won't be read if it doesn't show up in that search.

Some of this is intuitive. Instead of writing web copy for a furniture store using "davenport," an older industry term for a piece of furniture, use "sofa" or "couch." You can also use a helpful tool to find out what people are actually searching for using Google Trends. You can find generally what people are searching for currently, the preferred term for a specific topic or item, how search varies by time or geography, and more. For advanced training in SEO, consider taking a Google SEO course to get certified. But, whether you do it yourself or use an SEO tool, be sure that you can justify word choices in website copy based on *reader* perspective.

Halloween

This year, Halloween will fall on Wednesday, October 31st.

● Haunted house   ○ Corn maze   ● Pumpkin patch

Search interest in Halloween activities, past week

A Google Trends report on searches related to Halloween.

Landing pages are another strategic tool to use with web sites. A landing page is a simplified web page tied to something specific—a product launch, fundraising campaign, ballot initiative, and more. A landing page usually has a banner, a headline, some copy, and some links to additional information. It may link back to the main organization site, and vice versa. Landing pages work well to use as links in social media posts to help readers find that specific content quickly for the period of time it is being emphasized.

The last word on website writing is about design. There are professional software programs for website design, such as from Adobe. But there are also simpler programs that are free or less expensive. One of the more popular is WordPress, but others include Squarespace, Wix, and webs.com.

Blogs

The term blog comes from web log. In other words, blogs started as a form of online diary. They have evolved, but the primary features of blogs that distinguish them from websites is their generally personal tone, their assertion of opinion, and the organization of content. Simply, blogs contain a series of posts listed in reverse chronological order. That means the most recent post is on top and readers can scroll down to read progressively older posts.

There is variance in blogs, and corporate communications writers have decisions to make for organizational blogs. Should the blog be from one person, such as the CEO, in a personal tone of voice, or should it be more generically from the organization in an institutional, second-person ("we") voice? Should there only be one author, or multiple authors over time who each receive a byline and bio? The decision depends on everything from organizational culture, the nature of relationships between organization and publics, and the purpose of the blog. It is important to be strategic in these decisions, and stay consistent once they have been made.

There are several platforms for blogs, including WordPress, mentioned under websites, which is the most popular. Others include:

• <u>Type Pad</u>

• <u>Blogger</u>

• <u>Tumblr</u> (a micro blog site popular on mobile phones)

A good idea before starting your own blog is to research other blogs already out there that publish content in the same industry, product category, issue or topic. You can do so via Google blog search, but there are a few steps:

• First, navigate to a Google search page.

• Once on Google Search, click on the "News" tab near the top of the screen.

• Click the "Tools" button.

- Click the "All news" option and a dropdown menu will appear, with the options of "All news" and "Blogs". Select "Blogs".

- Now you can search all blogs being indexed by Google for any topic which you are interested.

When it comes to blog writing, you want to consider interactivity and dialogue, tagging, encourage subscriptions, allowing reader comment, sharing posts on social media and encouraging sharing. Here's a closer look at each of these aspects of blog writing.

Interactive. As in websites, but even more so, blogs should have many words that are hyperlinks to other content, either on the blog itself, the organization's own web site, or outside information (a source for a claim made on the blog, the bio of a person mentioned, the site of an organization mentioned, and so on). This not only is useful to readers, but it makes a blog rise up in search engines, and it could lead to reciprocal links to your blog from the other sites and blogs to which you linked.

In November 2011, at the National Communication Association annual conference, Corey Anton was awarded the "Best Book Award" by the Philosophy of Communication Division, for his book Sources of Significance: Worldly Rejuvenation and Neo-Stoic Heroism (Purdue University Press, 2010).

Tagging. Tags are keywords from a post that help others find it. WordPress and other blogging programs have a feature in which you can add tags with your post (and also include them when linking to the post on social media platforms). It is also possible to have categories for posts so that readers can find specific information in older posts quickly.

Tags

definition, history, PR, public relations

Subscriptions. A subscription to a blog helps readers get notified whenever there is a new post. It is a way to maintain regular readership as opposed to expecting viewers to keep searching or checking the blog to see if something is new. In other words, don't expect the readers to keep coming to the blog, make the blog go to them. People can receive an alert via email, follow your blog within

WordPress or other blogging platform, or use an RSS reader app for desktop or mobile phone. Subscriptions can be enabled within the blogging software platform or by using Real Simple Syndication (RSS).

Commenting, Dialogic. Allowing readers to comment on a blog is a difficult decision. Normally it's great because good public relations practice is to encourage transparency and two-way communication. But sometimes people are not civil in their own communication, or there are "bots" and other technologies that automate posts to blogs that are promoting another organization or cause, or a scam, and not related to content. For that reason it is wise to take a middle ground and allow moderated comments. That means you as blog author get an email when someone posts a comment and you need to approve it before it posts.

Another way to be two-way is to write with a dialogic voice in the way the blog is written. Essentially, a blog post should be more like a conversation than a proclamation. Academics have determined over the years that dialogic writing has five characteristics[8]:

• mutuality—it is obvious in the writing that the organization (or blog author) recognizes that there is a relationship between the organization and its publics;

• propinquity—evidence that interactions with publics can be spontaneous and in the moment;

• empathy—the organization understands and supports the public's goals and interests;

• risk—the organization is willing to interact with the public on the public's terms;

• commitment—the extent to which the organization dialogues, interprets and understands its interactions with its publics.

----

[8] Kent, M., & Taylor, M. (1998). *Building dialogic relationships through the world wide web. Public Relations Review,* 24(3), 324-334.

971k
Shares

Sharing. The next chapter is about social media. With regard to blogs, it is imperative that blog posts are shared by the blogging organization as well as shared by readers to expand each post's reach and the blogs subscriber base. It is simple to share each post on social media by connecting an organization's blog to each of its social media accounts. This can be done within the settings in WordPress and other platforms. But it is important to ensure that readers are encouraged to share posts on their own social networks. This can be done by adding a share button to each post, again within settings, or adding the code from Share This or Add This.

Analytics

As a final note regarding both web sites and blogs, it is important to think of the writing not as a product that is completed and done. Think instead of website and blog writing as a process—after writing, it is necessary to maintain, update, respond, share, reply, change and so on. One important aspect of this is to do the analytics, and adapt content accordingly.

Website and blog analytics can measure how many readers overall come to a site and each page or post. Analytics can show what content is most popular, how people are finding the site or content, how much sharing is going on, and other key metrics that can inform future writing.

Again, a lot of stats or analytics are built into the website content management system (CMS) or blogging platform software. But you can also use Google Analytics and add code to your site to gather detailed and useful information. Basic use is somewhat intuitive, but for those who want to be more advanced in their use of analytics, Google offers certification courses.

Checklist for Website and Blog Writing *(General persuasion in italics)*:

❑ *Grammar—punctuation and sentence structure are correct;*

❑ *Originality—no cliche's, jargon, platitudes;*

☐ *Appropriate—style, tone and voice relate to the purpose and audience (see below);*

☐ *Targeted—writing is implicitly and explicitly tailored to a specific public(s);*

☐ *Objective—the writing has an apparent purpose beyond mere information;*

☐ *Persuasive—there is a clear strategy in the writing intending to change attitudes and motivate behaviors.*

Plus:

☐ The writing is interactive and dialogic;

☐ The site or blog has easy navigation that is "outside-in";

☐ Writing uses word choices that are searchable (SEO);

☐ There is an option for readers to subscribe (RSS)

☐ It is possible for readers to comment (comments are replied to);

☐ The site/blog is mobile optimized;

☐ Content is shareable (social share links via AddThis or ShareThis)

Exercises:

1. Find a website AND a blog for an organization. Critique the writing and other aspects of websites and blogs described in this chapter.

2. Update the web site of your organization with a new home page, showing appropriate "outside-in" links on the navigation bar. Then go one click into the site (one of the links on the nav bar) and write more specific content there.

3. Start a blog for your organization. Determine if it will be written from the perspective of a person or organization. Write a post in the personal and dialogic style, as well as with other features described in this chapter.

CHAPTER 11: SOCIAL MEDIA

Social media is all the rage. It still seems new, although Twitter has been around since 2006. Facebook started in 2004 as a fad for college students and quickly became a global phenomenon. Other platforms soon proliferated, including LinkedIn, YouTube, Instagram, Snapchat and most recently TikTok.

Aside from the fun social media can be for personal use, it can be overwhelming and stressful when using social platforms for an organization. But for that reason, it is important to be strategic. Strategy for professional use of social media increases effectiveness and reduces stress. No organization can or should be on every platform. It is better to be on two, or three, or four and do really well at those, as opposed to being minimally present on many.

A good rule of thumb is to consider where your publics are, then what features a social platform has that work well for your organization, and where those factors intersect is where your organization should be on social media. For example, if you are primarily a business-to-business (B2B) company or have significant needs in employee recruitment, LinkedIn is the best place to be. If you have a highly visual story to tell about products or services, Instagram, Pinterest, and YouTube work well. If you want to reach a primarily younger audience, then Snapchat and TikTok are the rage.

The Social Paradigm

Social media posts look easy. They are short. Many people use them personally, so it would seem like a no-brainer to adopt one for a brand or nonprofit organization. But social media is more than just a new technology or platform to reach people. With social media came a change in the communication paradigm, or way of thinking. In other words, social media has its own culture when it comes to communicating between people, and between people and organizations. Much has been written about this shift, but it can be summarized briefly in three ways. With social media, communication with publics has gone from:

- Publication to *conversation*

- Channel to *network*

- Communication to *participation*

Conversation means that we are definitely two-way in our approach. On social media, people can and will talk back and expect a response. If organizations approach social media as just another megaphone to broadcast marketing messages, they will violate the expectations of people on social media and be unsuccessful, and possibly even counter productive.

A *network* as opposed to a channel means that communication between organizations and publics is not private, isolated or even two way. The organization is one "node" of many in communication, as if a person among many people in a group discussion.

Participation means an organization does not control conversations. It has to humbly enter in to conversations already existing, reply to the discussion already going on. Even when an organization starts a conversation, others can take it in new directions or themes.

Actually, savvy public relations professionals have always communicated in this way, even before there was internet or modern technology. It comes down to the attitude about the public, the desire to have transparent and ethical communication that works toward building relationships of mutual benefit. If that is the mindset of a professional communicator, social media will be a natural extension of communication. Others will definitely need to change their mindset and their writing.

So, the approach to social media can follow four steps. These steps can be followed each time one enters a social media platform or conversation, and it can be seen as the evolution of an organization's social media strategy over time. It is about not rushing in, being strategic, being humble and respectful of others, and ultimately being effective. The steps are as follows:

1. **Listen** to the conversation—monitor what's being said about your organization, or just the conversations in general;

2. **Respond** to the conversation—offer your opinion, perspective, and relevant information to the discussion, not trying to control but to offer something of value;

3. **Initiate** a conversation—by offering new information, you can start people talking in social media in other "rooms" (i.e. their networks); this is the multiplier effect of social media;

4. **Host** a conversation—use social media tools (chats, hashtags) as a forum for key constituents to talk, not just back and forth with the organization, but with each other.

Writing for Social Media

The first step in social media writing on behalf of an organization (after determining on which platforms you will focus) is to decide on your "voice." Will you be straightforward and informative, or will you go for a more personal, even human, tone in your posts? That depends on your reputational and relational goals. Either could be appropriate, but decide strategically and stick with it.

Even if the tone is more straightforward, a social media voice should still be personal and sound like a human. Also, it should not be entirely marketing or promotional in content. A rule of thumb is to maintain a 3:1 ratio of engagement and interactive messaging to bold promotional messaging. Notice the lighter touch to promotion by Dr. Pepper.

It is also important when writing for social media in a conversational mode that you can not only think of your own posts. You need to respond to others as well, whether it's light conversation or responding to serious customer service matters. Here too, the writing is what matters, the tone and timing as well as the content. See how Wendy's, which has a funny and edgy tone much of the time, responds to a customer complaint. Also note the strategy to move an angry person to a direct message (DM) to continue the conversation in private.

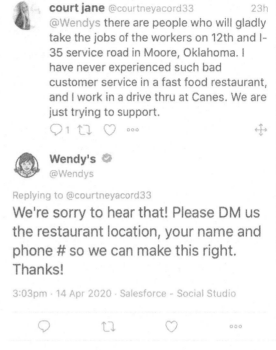

Since responding, replying and mentioning (tagging) is an important aspect of conversational writing in social media, it is necessary to have a good "follow strategy." This means seeking and following key publics—individuals and organizations—on social media so that you can see what they are posting and join in when appropriate. Also, the act of following others may encourage them to follow you. Putting those you follow on lists that make sense for your organization also works well. For example, customers, suppliers, donors, volunteers, partners, media, government, etc. On some platforms you can check the stream of just certain lists to isolate key types of content, or post only to select lists. On other platforms it is possible to construct public or private groups to have and host specialized conversations.

Now take a look at the specific writing conventions and tips for some specific platforms.

Twitter

- @reply. Show engagement by replying to others. This is the best kind of conversational engagement.

- RT = retweet. You can do this with or without comment. This is a way to share and support the comments of others, and doing so may encourage they do the same for your organization's posts.

- # for hashtags eg. #DrPepperfestival201. Hashtags can be used for a brand, product, event, hot topic, cause and more. Occasionally, they will trend and maximize exposure and engagement. They are also searchable for people to find relevant content quickly. Post hashtags on other tactics to make people aware to look for them.

- Chats for live online events.

- The voice and actor can be the organization, a person, or multiple people (using social media technology services covered at the end of the chapter). Consider if it's best to have one consistent voice or multiple, personal voices representing the organization on Twitter.

See _Twitter for Business_ for more tips and insights.

Facebook

- Use groups for intimate conversations with select people. They can be public or private. A Page is the public face of the brand, the 'account' on Facebook for an organization as opposed to a person.

- Tag people, share others' content and comment on theirs.

- Rich content has been proven to gain more views, likes, and shares. Use photos, videos, graphics and import blog posts and other content.

- Use stories as well as posts, which have a more timely storytelling feel than a post.

- Frequency= not too often, not too rarely. Generally speaking once or twice a day, at different times of day.

- Offer deals, incentives, solicit feedback, use polls and questions to engage people and gain responses.

See _Facebook for Business_ for more tips and insights. (Facebook also includes Instagram, Whats App).

LinkedIn

- Good especially for business-to-business, networking, employee recruitment

- Use company pages as a great way to reach out. People can see employees of your organization they might know.

- Generally LinkedIn has a more professional tone and the content is more professionally focused—resources, insights, solutions to business or organizational challenges, information about a profession or industry.

- Host or join groups which are organized by industry or professional interest. Post in them to reach specific key publics and be a thought leader.

Follow Jim

What are the success factors in a PR client/agency relationship? Here are 10 we've found ...

10 Habits of Successful Client/PR Agency Relationships
The math is simple: A good client + a good agency + the right attitudes = great PR ROI.
posted 1 month ago

Michael Smith 9 days ago · Good piece. For educators who do service-learning projects (where students provide PR services for area nonprofits), these tips ... »

See all 9 comments »

See LinkedIn Pages for advice on using LinkedIn for organizations.

Example of professionally relevant content on LinkedIn, with response.

YouTube

- Start an organizational "channel" for your video content.

- Share links or embed in other social media and blogs.

- Consider use of Tube Buddy (right), an extension and mobile app that offers templates and onboard keywords and more.

Advanced Keyword Research

Pinterest

- Visual emphasis, best for organizations that have photos and images, such as the humane society for nonprofits or a sporting good company.

- "Boards" are categories; "pins" are images.

- Pins can be saved to people's own boards, shared, or link to an organization website.

See Pinterest Business for more ways to use Pinterest as an organization.

Instagram

Instagram is owned by Facebook but appears as a separate social media site. It started as a photo sharing site and still primarily is, but users can do videos as well. The writing in posts with each image is important:

- Fill out brand profile information strategically so people can learn about you and go to your web site for additional engagement or transaction;

- What sort of messages about a brand do you want photos to convey?

- Think of yourself as a curator; decide which types of photos will engage your audience and not just what you want to promote.

- Always have your iPhone on hand to take photos.

- Add hash tags to all photos.

A non-profit Instagram post that tags a partner organization.

- Be innovative: contests, photos of company events, and other tactics engage people more than simple posts;

- Post on a regular schedule to maintain interest;

- Engage with others by commenting or clicking "like" on other photos. Respond to those who comment to you.

See the Facebook for Business link for Instagram information as well.

Snapchat

- Reaches younger demographic audience (for now);

- Many brands are there as well;

- High engagement is possible by using unique Snapchat features, such as filters and lenses

See Snapchat for Business for more on setting up a Snapchat account for organizational use.

Regardless of platform, there are some other considerations with regard to writing for social media. One is the notion of what makes a post "go viral." Related to that is the shelf-life of a post, how how long of a chance it has to be actually seen on different platforms before it is buried in the news feed. And finally, a practical consideration of image sizes for photos on social media.

With regard to virality, or what makes a post become increasingly shared and widely popular, academics and professionals have determined the following factors lead to an increased likelihood that a post really catches on:

- Psychological and sociological response in a person (remember the chapter on persuasive theory too that indicates when people respond);

- Shareability and memorability—if people remember it or *want* to share it, a post is likely to go viral. Often people share because a shared post is an extension of their own identity;

- Perceived value—again, the content of the post is valuable to the reader (not just the organization) in terms of information or entertainment;

- Inter-platform integration—the post can work on blogs and other social channels.

- Potential reach—obviously, if a platform has a lot of users and the followers of your organization have lots of followers, there is a greater chance of virality.

With regard to shelf life, on some platforms, a post is there and gone and if people aren't there at relatively the same time, they are not likely to see it. Others have more of a lengthy time and a post may be seen because they are not in real time but fed to a person according to likes, shares and so on. Here's a general estimate of how long content lasts on different platforms.

HOW LONG DOES YOUR CONTENT LAST?

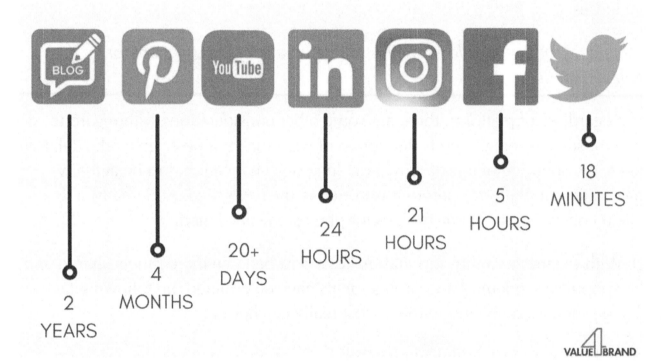

What this means is that a social media manager has to be engaged or online "in the moment" to post and respond and really engage people actively on Twitter in particular, a little less so on Facebook, and the other platforms give more time for a post to be seen. But even so, it is always important to be aware of responses to posts and not assume it will be seen by all followers each time.

Image size is also important to consider when posting photos and graphics on social media. This chart is a helpful way to remember it is not one size fits all.

Social Media Tools

While it is possible to log on to social media channels on a laptop or phone each time you want to post and monitor content, using a tool to schedule and organize posts and feeds can be very useful if you are on multiple platforms, with lots of content and engagement for an organization.

One of the top tools is an app that allows a larger view of columns for different accounts, notifications, posts and more of Twitter.

Network	Image Type	Size (pixels)
f	Cover Photo	851 x 315
	Profile Photo	300 x 300
	Posted Image	700 x 700
	Posted Link or Ad	1200 x 627
Instagram	Profile Photo	110 x 110
	Posted Photo	1080 x 1080
	Ad Photo	1080 x 1080
Pinterest	Profile Photo	165 x 165
	Posted Pin	735 x infinite
	Board Display	220 x 150
Twitter	Header Photo	1500 x 500
	Profile Photo	400 x 400
	In-Stream Photo	440 x 220
	Twitter Card	800 x 320
YouTube	Cover Photo	2560 x 1440
	Profile Photo	800 x 800
	Video Upload	1280 x 760
LinkedIn	Cover Photo	646 x 220
	Profile Photo	400 x 400
	Brand Logo	100 x 60
	Posted Photo	800 x 800

Hootsuite is a very popular industry standard tool that allows free use for a few platforms, and a paid version for more than that. This is also very helpful to plan and organize posts and monitor engagement. Whereas Tweetdeck only works for Twitter, Hootsuite allows multiple social platforms and blogs to be integrated.

There are other more professional, and therefore paid, options for social media management tools. One of the more popular ones is Sprout Social for its multiple features from posting to analyzing.

Finally, as with all corporate communications writing and public relations in general, evaluation is important. In social media, it is important to go beyond just counting followers and likes to look at engagement and conversations, as well as conversions, or when a social media engagement leads someone to do whatever the goal was—go to a web site, download something, fill out a form, order something and so on.

The social media platforms have onboard stats and analytics, and Google analytics as mentioned in the website and blog chapter can also measure social media.

Onboard analytics from top to bottom, LinkedIn, Facebook, Sprout Social.

Checklist for Social Media Writing *(General persuasion in italics)*:

☐ *Grammar—punctuation and sentence structure are correct;*

☐ *Originality—no cliche's, jargon, platitudes;*

☐ *Appropriate—style, tone and voice relate to the purpose and audience (see below);*

☐ *Targeted—writing is implicitly and explicitly tailored to a specific public(s);*

☐ *Objective—the writing has an apparent purpose beyond mere information;*

☐ *Persuasive—there is a clear strategy in the writing intending to change attitudes and motivate behaviors.*

Plus:

☐ The writing is interactive and dialogic;

☐ The writing is conversational and personal.

☐ The posts include replies, tags, mentions and shares of others' posts.

☐ The posts include videos, photos and images.

☐ Creative use of features of platforms, such as polls, hashtags etc.

Exercises:

1. Find the social platforms of an organization you like. Find them on several platforms. How are they different across platforms? Critique their posts according to the standards in this chapter for social media writing..

2. Come up with a social media plan for your organization. Which platforms will you use and why? Write five posts for each platform using a variety of features specific to each platform, and the content and writing style mentioned in this chapter. (You can use a simulator to see what posts would actually look like, using Zeoob or search for (name of platform + simulator).

CHAPTER 12: ANNUAL REPORTS

Annual reports are an important annual opportunity for organizations to communicate to a variety of publics. Public companies, those that sell stock, are required by the Securities and Exchange Commission (SEC) to produce an annual report as well as various quarterly and other documents.

There are two misconceptions about annual reports, however:

1. Annual reports are done by accountants, not PR people;

2. Annual reports are only needed by large public companies.

Both of these ideas are wrong. As will be shown in this chapter, annual reports are more than financial information and can be used as a creative and effective way of reaching a large variety of *stakeholders*, not just stockholders. A stockholder is only someone who has purchased stock in a company. A stakeholder is anyone who may be affected, financially or otherwise, by the success or failure of an organization.

That's why annual reports are also not just for public companies. Small, private businesses can and do publish annual reports. Nonprofit organizations and governmental bodies from the local to federal level can do annual reports as well.

Annual Report Purpose

In terms of corporate communications value, an annual report is more than financial communication and has more than a financial purpose. From a public relations perspective, the purpose of an annual report is three-fold:

• accountability —the annual report should be a reflection of the past year, stating what was accomplished and how stated objectives from the previous year have been completed or not;

• vision—an annual report should look ahead and state plans and goals for the coming year (the SEC prohibits "forward-looking statements" that predict specific increases in stock value);

• reputation—an annual report is a way to tell stories that illustrate an organization's vision, values and purpose.

In a sense, an annual report is an opportunity to tell the full story of an organization in a single tactic. The stories, the publics, and the purpose of the annual report will vary based on the type of organization. So it's best to consider corporate, nonprofit, and government annual reports separately.

Corporate Annual Reports

Corporate annual reports can either all look the same, or they can have tremendous variety. They all look the same because the SEC required form for an annual report is called a 10-K and they have mandated areas of information that public companies must report. So, the writing will be different, but 10Ks are black and white with the same subheads and categories of information, as shown in the example table of contents from a 10K.

THERMO FISHER SCIENTIFIC INC.
ANNUAL REPORT ON FORM 10-K
FOR THE FISCAL YEAR ENDED DECEMBER 31, 2017
TABLE OF CONTENTS

However, public companies can spruce up their annual report with color, photos and more creative writing in a separate report that accompanies the 10K, or by including the 10K within a colorful document called a "wrap."

These creative additions to the required annual report can be opportunities to tell stories, offer content not specifically outlined in a 10K, communicate to publics beyond just investors, and achieve broader goals having to do with reputation.

In addition to the 10K on the previous page, the same company produced this more colorful and creative report that touts its mission, innovation, and unique business practices.

Of course, non-public companies, also called private, are not required to produce an annual report. But they may want to do so as a public relations tool. Again, annual reports are not just for investors. Other publics of interest for a corporate annual report include employees, the local community, customers, government officials, and more.

Research by the National Investor Relations Institute (NIRI) and others have determined the content of a corporate annual report that really adds value and interest for readers naturally includes key business indicators:

• Key industry factors (competition, market share, issues);

• Customers (purchase motivation, distribution channels, penetration);

• Market growth drivers (new opportunities, geographic expansion);

- New product opportunities (developments, sale of new products);

- Intellectual property (patents, trademarks, unique employee capability);

- Strategic plan detail (key market opportunities, diversification, new tech);

- International business (performance, opportunities, issues);

- Margin (cost reduction, pricing strategies).

However, company annual reports are not all business. Businesses large and small are also doing sustainability reports, corporate social responsibility (CSR), reports, and diversity and inclusion annual reports. If the "bottom line" in financial terms refers to the bottom line of a financial statement, sustainability annual reports report on the "triple bottom line," which is economy, equity, and environment (the 3 Es) or in another way profit, people, and place (the 3Ps). Yet another term relative to corporate annual reports is ESG, which stands for environment, social, and governance, which have been proven to be three factors investors care about when making investing decisions. ESG characteristics have also been shown to lead to good long-term performance.

As an example, ABInBev, a global beverage company, has aligned its sustainability goals with the United Nationals Sustainable Development Goals and reports on them on its website.

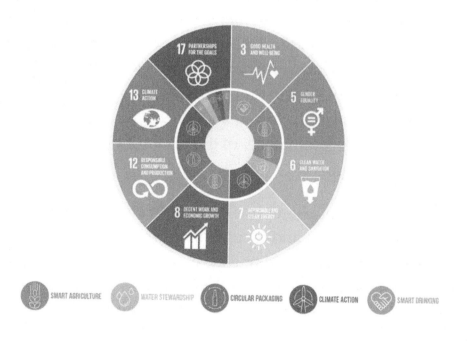

Reporting on a company's efforts and progress in the area of diversity and inclusion can be folded in to a CSR or sustainability annual report, but some companies do them separately, especially if they have articulated diversity as a key component of their corporate values and purpose and have a diverse set of stakeholders. For example, Kellogg publishes an annual diversity and inclusion annual report.

Nonprofit Annual Reports

Nonprofit organizations also do annual reports. They just have a different set of stakeholders. It is possible to say they have a different type of investor, namely donors, who invest in a nonprofit not to earn money but to make a difference and affect change on whatever the mission may be of the nonprofit they choose to support.

Nonprofit annual reports communicate accountability, vision and reputation to their publics too, just in a different way. Nonprofits are accountable to donors, that they spent charitable dollars received wisely and as they were intended. They communicate vision by stating what they see as a problem or cause, and how they have and will address it successfully. The reputation comes from being a thought leader on their cause or successful

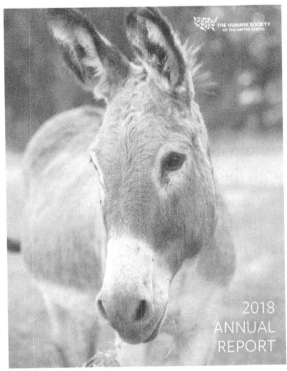

An annual report from the Humane Society

in their work.

The primary publics for nonprofit annual reports are donors, those who have received or need their services, volunteers and those who care about the nonprofit's cause, government leaders, potential institutional funders, partners with whom to work on their cause, and members of the community.

One compelling reason to produce a quality nonprofit report is because nonprofit tax and other financial information is online via guidestar.org. If key publics can access information about any nonprofit here from a third party, it makes sense to ensure an organization publishes its own as well to ensure accuracy and control messaging.

Government Annual Reports

A county health department annual report

Just as corporations are mostly accountable to investors, and nonprofits are mostly accountable to donors, government units and agencies are accountable to citizens or taxpayers. They therefore do annual reports to report on taxes received and how they were spent. Government annual reports can give an overview of initiatives completed in the past year, and plans for the year to come in their particular jurisdiction.

Governments can do annual reports for an entire unit of government, such as a city or county. Or they can produce annual reports on specific departments, such as a parks department, health department, or road commission.

A trend for government communication has been to make an online dashboard in addition to or in place of an annual report. As the name implies, a dashboard is not done just once a year, but is continually updated with new data on key metrics, such as number of park visitors, the cost of road paving or anything officials think citizens want to or have a right to know. Government dashboards can be produced by companies such as iDashboards, who take data and present it in an easy-to-understand graphical depiction.

Writing Annual Reports

When it comes to writing annual reports, it is important to keep in mind that some content will be very straightforward, i.e. not very creative, such as financial data or other key facts to report. Meanwhile, there are other places where an annual report can benefit from the creativity of the writer.

One area of creativity for an annual report is to give the report each year a unique *theme*. The theme should be obvious on the cover, both in words and design. Then the theme can be carried out in the letter from the president, the table of contents, stories and other content within, as well as the design.

For example, a popular national chain restaurant whose stores were always visible from the highways across the country had an annual report one year called "road trips." The report used images of road signs and highways, and the copy used words like "exit," "accelerate," and "off-ramp."

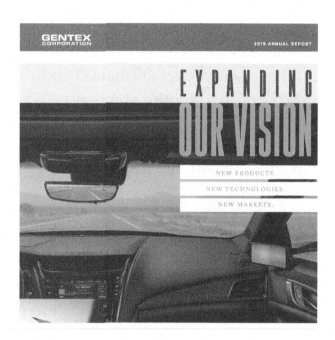

A company annual report with a theme in text and graphics, as well as contents inside.

Most annual reports will start with a letter from the CEO, president, mayor or whomever is the most significant leader of the entity publishing the report. This is where the tone can be more personal, in first-person voice, with the writing more creative and visionary (within SEC guidelines if a public company), and can establish the theme and set the tone for the report. Generally speaking, the author of the letter should reflect on the past year's accomplishments and even disappointments, then speak to the future year to come and the goals and plans. All of this could creatively incorporate the theme.

Some annual reports are written as magazines. They come out once a year and include a series of feature stories that collectively tell the story of what happened in the past year. Financial information and other lists of facts could be included, but the emphasis is on stories.

A sample outline for an annual report that could be used in annual reports for a company, a nonprofit and a government is shown here. Note they can vary of course based on the size and specific context of the organization.

Annual report outline:

• Cover introduces theme concept—in words and design

• Theme concept can be carried inside in words and design

• Table of contents

• Letter from President, board chair (should be personal and based on theme)

• Roster of board members and staff

• Creative articles, copy that highlights key thing—events, accomplishments etc-- from past year

• Financial information, charts and graphs

Note that in nonprofit annual reports, it is wise to publish a list of donors (unless donors wished to give anonymously). It is common to set up tiers or levels of giving by certain amount, even giving names to each level and listing donors in those categories. This gives special honor to larger gifts and may encourage others to give or give more in subsequent years. In addition to listing donors, it is a good strategy to profile some donors, letting them tell why they give and believe in the cause and have faith in the organization.

Checklist for Annual Report Writing *(General persuasion in italics)*:

- ☐ *Grammar—punctuation and sentence structure are correct;*

- ☐ *Originality—no cliche's, jargon, platitudes;*

- ☐ *Appropriate—style, tone and voice relate to the purpose and audience (see below);*

- ☐ *Targeted—writing is implicitly and explicitly tailored to a specific public(s);*

- ☐ *Objective—the writing has an apparent purpose beyond mere information;*

- ☐ *Persuasive—there is a clear strategy in the writing intending to change attitudes and motivate behaviors.*

Plus:

- ☐ The annual report has a theme;

- ☐ The theme is clear on the cover in words and design, and carried through the report;

- ☐ The letter from the CEO/President is personal and both reflective of the past year and looking ahead to the next, all applying the theme creatively;

- ☐ A table of contents shows a logical plan for the report and follows the outline from this chapter;

- ☐ The writing demonstrates accountability and vision and builds reputation.

Exercises:

1. Find an annual report of a company, nonprofit or government online. Critique it according to the annual report criteria for contents and writing explained in this chapter.

2. Plan an annual report for your organization. Come up with a theme, write the letter from the executive and a table of contents to show how the theme would be carried out and what contents you would include in the report.

Part III—Measuring Corporate Communication

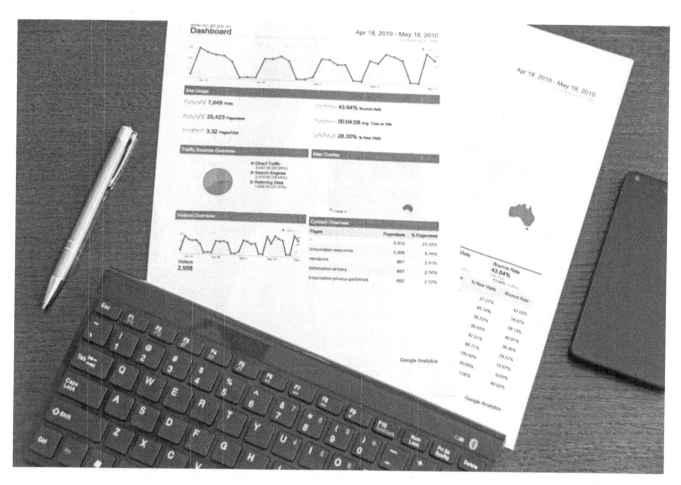

So you've done all this writing, and you think it's really good! But, so what? How do you know if your corporate communication writing is effective or not? It all depends on measuring the right things in the right way.

CHAPTER 13: EVALUATION

The key to good evaluation of public relations of any kind, and therefore of corporate communications writing, is what you actually measure. What you should measure was discussed in chapter 3 on communication audits and plans.

Essentially, good corporate communications writing meets the objectives that were established at the outset. And a good objective has to do with what the public does in response to our writing. This is called an "outcome" objective.

Some communicators make the mistake of setting what are called "output" objectives. These are objectives for what they want to do, such as distribute 500 brochures, or add a page to the web site. That just means planning to do tactics.

It really is all about the response of the target publics. And generally the public responds to corporate communications writing with a change in one of three things, called the "3 As": awareness, attitude or action.

Methods of Evaluation

There are several methods of evaluation, ranging from basic to advanced. The advanced methods get at measuring outcome in the intended public. But we will consider them all here, from production, to exposure, to outcome. Finally, we'll look at measuring relationships.

Production

This is simply a measure of what was produced by the communication professional. It's a good way to be accountable to a boss or client, but not very complete in terms of measuring whether the writing was successful.

Methods of production measurement include tear sheets of ads that ran, copies of news releases, and sample copies of brochures or other tactics.

Exposure

Exposure is a measure of how many people were 'exposed' to or saw your message. This is a little more insight than production. However, knowing that people saw a message does not tell us how they reacted.

Methods of measuring exposure include news monitoring services that show news articles or broadcasts stories. You can also do this yourself with a Google news search. Looking at the number of hits and visitors to a web site, or counting followers and shares on social media are another way. Exposure from advertising has traditionally been measured by calculating gross ratings points (GRPs), which multiplies the reach (number in an audience or subscribers) times the frequency (the number of times an ad runs).

A controversial (see Barcelona Principles later) method for measuring exposure is to equate news publicity or earned media to advertising in terms of cost, called advertising value equivalency (or AVE). In other words, if you send a news release that results in an article that takes up a quarter of a page of a newspaper, and a quarter-page ad would have cost $500, the ad equivalency of the media relations is $500. This is a way to put media relations exposure in financial terms, but it is frowned on by most professionals because it does not demonstrate actual exposure or response, nor does it account for the fact that news is different than ad content in terms of credibility and interest level.

Other ways to measure exposure include embedding evaluation techniques into tactics. This might include a unique url or 800-number so you know anyone using them is responding to a tactic and therefore must have seen it. In a similar way, counting reply envelopes from a direct mail package or those who attend an event is an observed form of exposure.

Outcome

As noted, measuring outcomes in terms of response by the public is the gold standard. This is also the hardest in some ways, because how can we know if someone is aware or how they are thinking? Action can be observed or reported.

So, a typical measurement technique for outcome is to conduct a pre-post survey to see if targeted publics experience a change in awareness, attitude, or action as a result of communications. However, outcomes can be observed based on publics communicating in response or observed behavior or sentiment (opinion) in emails, social media or other visible communication by the publics.

Relationships

Some might say it is hard to measure relationships. But organization-public relations have been shown to be measurable by academic research and in professional practice[9] on four levels often checked with a survey in which a target public is asked about these items in relation to an organization:

- Trust—the degree to which they trust the organization;

- Satisfaction—how satisfied they are with the organization's communication with them;

- Commitment—how much the sense the organization is committed to their well-being and a relationship with them;

- Control mutuality—the degree to which they feel they have as much control over communications with the organization as does the organization.

Barcelona Principles

As a final note, the Barcelona Principles are a set of global communication evaluation standards established by a meeting of many professionals and academics in Barcelona, Spain in 2010. The standards were updated slightly in 2015. The principles include:

1.Goal setting and measurement are fundamental to communication and public relations and should always be done;

2.Outcomes are the type of objective that should be measured, not only output;

3.Business results, or the effect on the performance of the whole organization, should be measured, not only communication tactics and goals;

4. Quantity AND quality are important and useful methods of evaluation, for example, not just number of responses but sentiment;

---

[9] *Hon, L.C. and Grunig, J.E. (1999). Guidelines for measuring relationships in public relations. Institute for Public Relations.* www.instituteforpr.org

5.Ad Value Equivalencies are NOT the value of PR or communication, as noted above;

6.Social media can and should be measured along with other tactics;

7.Transparency and replication are important, meaning we should show how we measure and demonstrate that it is valid and not inappropriately interpreted.

In summary, if you measure in this way, and you can demonstrate that your corporate communications have accomplished an objective that caused a meaningful change in an intended public in a way that meets an overall organizational goal, then you are a successful corporate communications writer.

Made in the USA
Monee, IL
13 January 2022

88823537R00066